The Journeys of
DAVID TOBACK

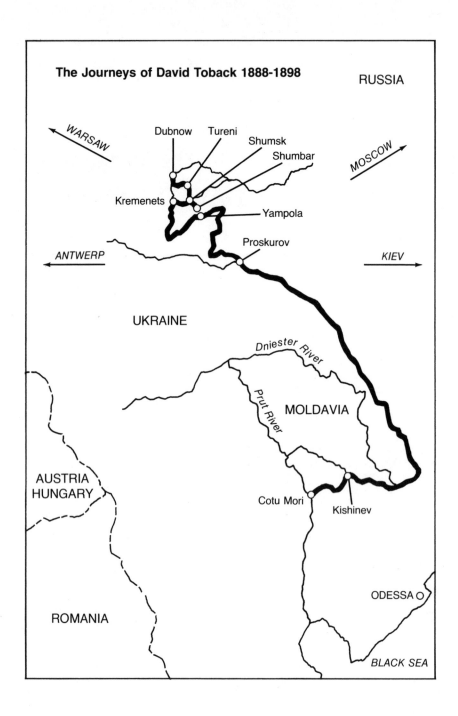

The Journeys of David Toback 1888-1898

The Journeys of
DAVID TOBACK

As retold by his granddaughter
CAROLE MALKIN

SCHOCKEN BOOKS · NEW YORK

First published by SCHOCKEN BOOKS 1981
10 9 8 7 6 5 4 3 2 1   81 82 83 84
Copyright © 1981 by Carole Malkin

Library of Congress Cataloging in Publication Data

Malkin, Carole.
The journeys of David Toback.

"Based on the English translation of the Author's grandfather's
unpublished Yiddish memoir."
1. Toback, David.   2. Jews in Russia—
Biography.   3. Jews in the United States—
Biography.   4. Russia—Biography.   5. United
States—Emigration and immigration—Biography.
I. Title.
DS135.R95T635   947'.004924 [B]   80-22962

Designed by Nancy Dale Muldoon

Manufactured in the United States of America

ISBN 0-8052-3756-9

DEDICATED TO
Richard Malkin
William Dickey
and
Konstantin Berlandt

Contents

Illustrations

THIS BOOK is based on an English translation of an unpublished Yiddish memoir by David Toback. The five notebooks from which it was drawn have been donated by Carole Malkin, his granddaughter, to the Jewish National Library in Jerusalem.

The Journeys of
DAVID TOBACK

David at his butchershop on New York's Lower East Side. This picture was taken shortly before he sat down to write his memoirs.

I begin to write my memoirs

NEW YORK CITY, ARMISTICE DAY, 1933

WHEN I OPENED my eyes this morning, the first thought in my head was that it was the anniversary of my daughter's death. She was a woman with small children. A year ago she jumped from the roof of a building. The sorrow pinches my heart.

After I said the morning prayers, I started to pace around this room as if I could make the pain go away. From one end to the other I walked, and there on the kitchen table was the pile of composition books I bought four months ago. At that time I decided that since I am retired I should write something about the remarkable life I have led, about how and why I came to America in 1898. After all, thousands immigrated with me at the same time, so maybe it would have some importance to examine the life of one individual.

The notebooks are already covered with dust. I try not to notice them. Even with my eyes closed I'm reproaching myself. I used to work eighteen hours in twenty-four as a presser of boys' pants, and it was even worse when I owned a butcher store. But now what do I do? Nothing. I have the time and I have no excuse.

Why shouldn't I be able to write? My entire life I have been scribbling little notes here and there. From my butcher store housewives went home with whole speeches written on the paper in which their chickens were wrapped. There are hundreds of stories I want to tell. But each time I try to write, I can't get a word out. Either my head is a blank and I wander over and sit by the window instead, or just as I dip the pen in the ink my hand starts to tremble.

Just now, my wife came in and saw me communing with the notebooks. A look of disgust came over her face.

"*Nah*, put it away already. I should have my table."

"Here the books will stay."

"Why? You'll never do anything with them."

I said nothing, just went to sit down and took the pen in my hand. I wrote down the date, the anniversary of my child's death, and suddenly I realized that today I would truly begin my book. The year of mourning is over. Now I will try to drive away the bad thoughts by remembering everything I can about my youth in Russia.

I become a Jew

SHUMBAR AND SHUMSK, 1875–1889

I WAS BORN in 1875, the son of Leibish Hershik and Chaya Sarah. Don't think it is an easy thing to be born a Jew. Under Czar Nicholas there was a reign of terror. Edict after edict was issued against us. We were not supposed to do this, or travel here, or do business in that—the faster we thought of ways to keep a crust of bread in our mouths, the czar and his court thought of some way of snatching it away. We, the Jews, were the chosen and the despised people.

Yet, among persecuted people arise individuals of the greatest pride. My mother was one of these. The larger our troubles, the straighter she held her tall, slender body. Her black eyes could burn you up alive. They shone like live coals in her pale face. My father never looked at her directly. He always hung his head. He was a redhead with sunken cheeks, watery eyes, a large beak nose, and a thick, curly beard. There was usually a cigarette between his lips.

His profession was that of miller. Since Jews were not permitted to own property, he would rent a mill from a Russian landlord. Each of his enterprises failed, and we moved around a lot from one small village in the Ukraine to another, always hoping he would have better luck. These villages were all alike, small places with a few hundred people, with a potter, a blacksmith, and a beekeeper.

The mills were thin and high with onion-shaped tops like the cupolas of churches. They were built a little apart on top of a high hill to catch the wind.

Usually we were the only Jews, and I played with the peasant children and was one of them. We amused ourselves with all kinds of games; sometimes we pretended we were bears, and sometimes we were wolves running through the snow. We played hide and seek. They told me the stories they heard from their grandmothers about witches and forest spirits, and I believed every word. There was no school, of course. How could there be a school or even a book in such places? Would oxen want to read? All day the peasants worked on the soil and at night they slept. Nothing more. So why should there be a book?

When I reached the age of six, my parents began to consider it the greatest hardship that I had not yet begun a religious education, and they managed to lure various tutors to stay with us. None of them stayed for long, and none of them taught me much. I knew more about the sting of a switch than the aleph-bet.

I had one who was so vicious that the peasants where we lived attacked him and pinched him all over his body the way they had observed him doing to me. The tutor had been dragging me down the road, and they rescued me from his tortures. One of them, called Chavder, held me in his arms and called me *Nash* David, which means "our David." The others kicked the tutor and called him "Yid."

Each time we moved, it was with fewer wagons to carry our possessions. The only thing that grew was the size of our family. By the time I was twelve years old and we had come to settle in the village of Shumbar, I had three brothers and two sisters. The eldest in the family was Hindah. I was the next oldest, and then came my sister Shivah and my brothers Beryl, Heschel, and Yossel. Eight of us lived in a small peasant log cabin. There was a tiny entrance hall, a storeroom on one side of it, and on the other a dwelling room with a clay stove against a whole wall. The stove had ledges and almost went up to the ceiling. In the winter we slept on the ledges, or as close as we could get to the warmth. For furniture we had only a large table, two chairs, and a bench that went around two of the walls.

My father had become so poor that he could no longer pay a tutor's wages. To me it did not seem entirely a hardship that I had to prepare for my bar mitzvah alone. I wanted to make my parents proud, and I worked hard.

The morning of my bar mitzvah arrived in March of 1888, a freezing cold one. When I awoke, my father gave me a pair of *te-fillin** to put on for the first time. These *tefillin* were 132 years old, and I was the fifth generation to receive them.

My father said, "My child, many Jews consider your great-grandfather a *tzaddik*† and wish they could possess the *tefillin* that belonged to him. Recently a rich man, Alter Richels, who lives in Shumsk, the same town as your grandmother, offered me one hundred rubles if I would give them to him. You know how poor we are and how we could have used the money. I refused. Value these *tefillin*. Each day you pray with them, they will help you to attain the pure thoughts and the good deeds of your ancestors."

The bar mitzvah ceremony was held at a neighbor's, several versts‡ away. Jews had come from the little villages around so there would be enough for a *minyan*,§ and there was a visiting rabbi. I was dressed in my usual rags and instead of boots had strips of cloth wrapped around my feet. My mother and brothers and sisters stayed at home because their clothes were even less decent than mine. After the services I ran back to them and found my mother weeping because she had not the means to make me a party in celebration of the day.

How astonished and happy we were that night when all those who had been at the services came to our home. People had decided in advance to all contribute a little and make a banquet in my honor. They carried pots of potatoes and cabbage, roasted lamb, and big loaves of bread. There were not enough places for ev-

---

* Phylacteries.
† Holy man; saint.
‡ One verst is equivalent to 3,500 feet.
§ Quorum; the ten male Jews required for religious services.

eryone to sit, but still we managed to arrange ourselves and were about to say the blessing. Suddenly we heard the sound of horses' hooves.

Everyone rushed outside, and in the distance we saw four black horses pulling a large coach. In our village of Shumbar, which was such a tiny, poor place, people traveled by sleigh or by wagon, never by coach. To us it was like an apparition drawing closer. The horses pulled up before us and out of the coach stepped several Hasidim in long black kaftans, with fur hats, thick beards, and curled *peyes.*°

Alter Richels, the tallest one, a man with white hair and beard but an unlined face, approached my father.

"Greetings, Leibish Hershik. Last month I offered to buy your *tefillin,* but you refused. You know how much I revere and honor your grandfather who wore them. When I heard that his great-grandson would put them on for the first time today, I and several of my friends decided to come and witness this event ourselves. Congratulations to you on your son's bar mitzvah."

He introduced his companions. Even in our village we had heard of such holy men as Reb Israel Rishiner and Reb Mordechai Tchernobler, the rulers of Hasidic courts. Along with them was a *rav,*† an elderly man with kind eyes, whose reputation was even more awesome.

My father invited everyone into our small home. The villagers were reluctant to enter. They were uneducated and dressed peasant-style with short coats and baggy trousers, so how could they hold their heads up? Silent veneration filled them. They trembled to be near such scholars. Still when they were urged, they dared not refuse.

Imagine the kindness of these Hasidim, that they spoke to everyone in a friendly way, that they began to discourse on Torah. Their faces shone happily as if our poor cabin were the richest home. I understood only a little of what they said and yet I felt moved, as did others around me. These village Jews were strong

° Sidelocks.
† Rabbi.

men who lifted heavy loads and pulled wagons, but they had tears streaming down their cheeks—and just imagine the women.

Suddenly, as if I too were a learned scholar, the *rav* addressed me, saying he heard I had studied *Nezekin** in the Mishnah, and he wished to examine me. At first I could not believe he meant me and I looked about to see if there was someone else he wanted to come forward. He kept staring at me and nodding, so I got up and went toward him, barely bringing one foot in front of another. My face was burning and my heart thumping so hard that I did not understand how it stayed in my chest.

The *rav* put his hand out to me and whispered, "Don't be afraid."

The moment he touched me I felt a little calmer. I noticed my mother staring at me and suddenly I felt confident that I could answer anything he asked—and that was how it happened. For each question a response would leap into my head and begin to develop, first one way, then another. All the ideas I thought of were new to me. I could hardly believe how quiet everyone was and how they stared at me, and I sensed it was with great respect. This was particularly so when the *rav* stood up, came over to me, and kissed me on the forehead.

My mother's joy was extreme. She was unable to contain herself and flung herself on me and began to weep. For a long time she clutched me to her and could not be torn away. Finally the other women were able to calm her with soothing words and caresses.

The *rav* addressed her and my father in a solemn tone. "Your child is not an ordinary person. Not only is he intelligent, but he has a pure heart. You must see to it that he studies with good teachers, even if you have to send him away from you."

He and his companions prepared to leave, and everyone followed them when they went out. A silver crescent lit the night. Thousands of stars danced around me, and I felt as if I were floating.

Alter Richels whispered in my ear, "You see what wonderful *te-*

---

* "Damages"; a division or "order" of the Mishnah dealing with civil and criminal law. The Mishnah, a section of the Talmud, consists of a collection of oral laws.

fillin you have. Today, all of us have traveled far just for their sake. We wanted to see the child who would wear Reb Mentchel's *tefillin.* You will see, now that you have worn them, your whole life will change."

We watched the coach drive off until the tiny black dot it was disappeared.

Several weeks later a peddler passed through the village with a package from Alter Richels. My father gave it to my mother. We all gathered around as she opened it with trembling fingers. We received a coat for my mother and a pair of boots for me. Tucked into the toe of one boot were a few rubles and a letter. I read it aloud. Alter Richels said that maybe I should go to live with my grandmother in Shumsk where there was a Bes Medresh.*

Now I was to see how deeply the *rav*'s words impressed my parents. They discussed the letter constantly. Late into the night they whispered about my fate. Finally they informed me I would leave for Shumsk as soon as possible.

I began to cry piteously. I did not want to be torn away from my family, from everything I knew.

"You'll be with your grandmother," my mother comforted me.

I felt a little better until my father said, "You've been without a tutor too long. Now you'll have a teacher again."

What if I fell into the hands of another cruel teacher? "Can't I learn by myself here?" I pleaded.

"A *tzaddik* advised us to send you away. Do you want to go against the *rav*?"

I did not know what to answer. I bit my lips and tried to hold the sobs back.

Nothing would dissuade my parents, even their own unhappiness. I know at night that my mother cried to herself. My father was smoking more cigarettes than ever. One afternoon he came home and said he had heard that a Jew from the next village was driving to Shumsk. Two days later I was awakened early and taken out to where Yitzi Velvel waited with his wagon. I climbed on

---

* House of Study.

with my few belongings. My father shook my hand, and my mother hugged me. Hindah gave me a few cookies, and each of the other children gave me a small present—a kopeck, a wooden top, a quill.

Yitzi said, "It will be nighttime by the time you're finished. Let's go."

He snapped his whip and we drove down the road. I looked toward the horizon and wondered what I would find in the new life that awaited me.

We drove into a town with a few streets, a large marketplace, and rows of wooden houses of one and two stories, with shutters on the windows and small porches in front. Everywhere there were Jews. Shumbar had fewer than three hundred people and only about fifteen Jews who lived scattered here and there. In Shumsk there were nearly two thousand Jews, the men in knee pants with high white stockings or in long black kaftans, and the married women with *shaytlech** over their shaved heads.

It did not take long for my grandmother Esther to hear I had arrived. She came running down the street, not caring that she was splashing mud over her skirt and long white apron. She was an old woman with yellow skin, a bumpy nose, and a jaw that jutted forward. Her eyes looked wide open because her brows and lashes had been singed in a fire and had never grown back. Immediately she started to pat me with her bony, twisted hands and tears of joy came to her eyes that I had come to her. Every gesture showed her simplicity and kindness and eased my anxieties.

She led me to her spotlessly clean house of two rooms. To me it was a wonder that she had so much furniture—a bed, a table, chests, chairs, and even a big cabinet in which she had great valuables such as flowerpots, china dishes, and, best of all, a clock.

Before I could examine these treasures as fully as I desired, she had sat me down and begun to serve me a meal. I took a few bites and felt sick. Poor Grandmother could not cook. Her boiled potatoes were stones; her pancakes lay on a plate like a thick clay, and

---

* Plural of *shaytl*, the wig traditionally worn by married women.

even worse was her kasha, which was cold with a thick, greasy skin on the top. But what could I do? She was watching me anxiously and I did not want to hurt her feelings, so I had to keep swallowing.

Night came and I was to see that in town one had to sleep in a more refined way. I would have liked a pile of soft straw like the one I slept on at home, but my grandmother took out a trunk for my bed. All night I was pained by its hardness and was afraid I would fall off. It was not until dawn that I was exhausted enough to fall asleep—and just as I drifted off there was a loud banging at the door. I was so startled that I fell off the trunk and screamed to my grandmother that there were robbers breaking in.

She came and informed me, "Don't you know that Beryl the *shammes** comes to wake everyone up? Usually he knocks three times; but if someone has died, he knocks only twice at each house."

I washed, got dressed, and went outside. There I saw several boys. I thought I would make friends easily as I had done with the children in the village.

"Good morning," I greeted them. "My name is David."

"Don't lie, your name is Wormy Plums," answered a tall one in a shiny, new black coat who seemed to be the leader. The others called him Gur Aryeh.

"Get out of here, goy," he told me.

"I'm a Jew," I said, but they did not believe me. They were dressed in long gaberdines and had long, curled *peyes*, but I was wearing peasant clothes like a Russian.

As I was trying to decide whether to argue with them or run away, a rock hit me in the shoulder. It nearly knocked me down, and the place where it hit was burning. A whole barrage started, and now I didn't have trouble making up my mind. I ran as fast as I could. My heart was pumping so hard, I felt it would burst.

I was chased to the river on Shumsk's outskirts, then back to the center where there was a ruined fortress, and there I ran from behind one crumbling wall to another, and then out along the street

* Sexton.

again until I came to the Bes Medresh, a stucco building, larger than the others in the town. I rushed inside. There I sat in one corner panting, and I can imagine how pale and disheveled I looked. I decided to stay because I knew the boys dared not come in here to attack me. Probably they waited at the door.

Gradually I calmed down. The Bes Medresh was like another world. There were only a few high windows, so the light was dim. The floor was black flagstone. There were benches and tables of dark wood, and stall chairs built into the walls. Covering half the ceiling was the balcony belonging to the women's section. On every side I heard the buzzing of voices. I saw men moving about like shadows—some studying, some praying, and some talking.

The largest gathering, right near me, consisted of several *kest kinder*. These were young men between the ages of fifteen and thirty who were married but did not need to work because their fathers-in-law had contracted to support them as part of the marriage settlement. The only obligation of these young men was to study Torah, but much went on at the Bes Medresh besides praying and studying. These *kest kinder* would discuss their business deals; they had pooled their dowries and lent out at high interest and in this way made thousands of rubles. One such deal was being whispered about at the moment.

A young man from this group looked over at me and became curious. He left his friends and approached me.

"Why are you shivering? Are you frightened of us?"

I said, "I'm not."

I did not feel like confiding in him, but I changed my mind when I saw my enemies coming in and smirking at me. Gur Aryeh patted his pocket in a conspicuous way and I knew it was rocks that made it bulge out. I tugged on the sleeve of the *kest kind* who was just leaving and tried to think of some clever thing to say to keep him with me.

"I'll tell you why I'm afraid. It's because this morning I discovered an amazing fact about this town."

"Well, what is it?"

"That everything in Shumsk is the opposite of what it should be. Even the story about Adam and Eve must be different here."

The *kest kind* started to laugh and motioned his comrades over to be entertained too—and with such a crowd I felt a little more secure. In a loud voice I said whatever came into my head. I only hoped to keep the men around me.

"You see how it is. In the small village I come from we have dogs that bark and we throw rocks at them. But here all is reversed. Here it is the dogs that hurl the rocks. And what large ones they are capable of throwing! I have barely escaped with my life. There was such an enormous barrage that if I was hit just once it was only because these dogs have little skill. It was lucky they were Jewish instead of Christian dogs, who have better aim."

As I gave this speech I looked over at the boys, and the *kest kinder* comprehended my message.

One young man said, "We will see to it that our Jewish dogs are more courteous."

My attackers, who were so bold a little before, now hung their heads in shame. They crept over to the study tables and took out some books as if to read, but really to hide behind. There were a few who were angry I had exposed them, and when the *kest kinder* were not observing I got some threatening glances. In particular, Gur Aryeh resented me.

Later I learned that his grandfather was Alter Richels, and when this man who had taken such an interest in me arrived at the Bes Medresh he was soon informed of all that had happened.

He took Gur Aryeh aside and started to talk to him. Soon after, the boy came to me with red eyes and acted as meekly as possible. I felt his repentance was sincere. We sat down together and began to read and memorize from the same book. He took a few cookies out and gave them all to me. He told me I had been sent his old boots and he had an extra shirt he would give me as well. We started acting in a friendly way to each other. Alter Richels glanced over at us with a smile, and I could see by Gur Aryeh's expression that he worshiped his grandfather and would do anything to please him.

Later he confessed to me that he had gotten the other boys to attack me because he had heard his grandfather praise me on the speech I had made on the day of my bar mitzvah, and he was jealous. This astonished me. How could he be jealous of me when he had so much? He was intelligent, rich, well treated, and all the other boys admired him greatly.

Some of the *kest kinder* came over and started to examine me on Talmud. People were impressed with what I had achieved myself. One man predicted, "This boy is going to be a prodigy." There were no teachers in the Bes Medresh. Everyone learned by himself, and if you had a bit of trouble, you asked someone. It was the custom here for a less competent boy to study with one who was better in his studies. This way there was always someone at his side to whom he could bring his questions. As soon as it was suggested that I might be a prodigy, the fathers started competing among themselves that I should study with their child. Now, thanks to Alter Richel, I was well accepted by all, and everyone was petting me.

I could have studied with anyone, but I looked around and saw a boy sitting apart from everyone in the corner.

"Who is that? and why is he all alone?"

It was explained to me that his father was dead and his two older brothers were his guardians. They had prepared him for the draft with a hideous rash on his head—and four years ahead of when a medical exemption was needed. It was Shmuel Shocket's misfortune that he always stank. Other people avoided him.

The pain the boys had caused me was fresh in my mind, and I took pity. I went to sit with him. We opened a book and studied.

By the end of the day I was reconciled to these Jews. I too was a Jew studying in the Bes Medresh. I had friends. My education had begun. Gur Aryeh had decided he was going to give me a long coat which he had outgrown and advised me to let my *peyes* grow longer. I immediately agreed this would be for the best.

In Shumsk I became more and more of a Jew. Even the way I talked changed. I gestured more, and I was livelier. I was doing the things Jews did. All week I studied at the Bes Medresh, but on Sunday I went to the Shumsk market, a big cobblestoned square, and learned to do business and bargain just like almost everyone else in the town.

What a spectacle the market was! The peasants, dressed in their best, came in flaming red trousers and blue coats and carried staffs or had sabers. The women wore green wool jackets or colorful vests and black skirts covered with embroidery with petticoats showing at the hem. They wore head scarfs, but some had turbans, as did most of the men.

At six in the morning the first wagons appeared, and soon they packed the road so that one could scarcely move. The horses neighed and flicked their tails at flies. The peasants brought in fresh produce to sell the Jews in exchange for supplies, and their wagons were filled with dark red beets, green cabbages, potatoes, and onions. Others had cages with cackling, fat chickens. The Shumsk hawkers buzzed around the peasants with their dry goods and cried, "I will sell it to you cheap"; if they got pushed away they just came back again, tore at clothes, and pleaded more insistently.

There were terrible fights for bargains. Two women would pull off each other's kerchiefs and scratch at each other because both wanted the same quart of beans. Then the men arrived to take up their wives' defense. Here and there was a bloody nose, a split lip, or a black eye.

On market days I was up early to help my grandmother wheel over her wagon filled with soap, kerosene, dried fish, salt, and matches. I stood beside her, and she had in me a loud voice to proclaim her wares.

I always greeted the peasants warmly. Sometimes there were ones I recognized from the villages where I had lived and there was quite a reunion. They still called me *Nash* David. My grandmother would let me off so I could go about with them arm in arm.

One time I was walking like this and we saw a big crowd gathered by the house of my grandmother's neighbor, Abraham Moshe Lipsche. Lipsche and his wife were big wheat merchants who drove around to the Russian nobility and bought up grain and then resold it to the mills and the army. They did business in the thousands of rubles, but on the market day could not let a peasant go by who had even a single sack of grain without bargaining with him for it.

"What's going on? Why is there such a crowd?" we asked, and were informed Mrs. Lipsche had been caught giving short weight to a peasant. The constable had been called. I began to feel uneasy. I saw Jews being shoved and soon there was a division in the crowd. Peasants muttered and glowered on one side, and Jews stood apart and were silent, except for a few murmurs.

"Now all Jews will suffer. It was bad enough already, but when this story spreads it will be terrible for a Jew to go through a village."

"If only they had stolen a couple of horses. That the goyim* understand; it's what they themselves do. It would not do so much harm to Jews as this fiasco."

"Lipsche should be a nice, clean sacrifice for a goose's asshole."

One of my peasant companions said, "A wolf catches until he is caught." I started to answer him, but he refused to look at me. Another muttered, "Filthy Yids."

Without a word I went over to be with the Jews.

At this moment the constable, along with his deputies, arrived. Now the constable was a man with a red, conceited face, a long moustache that he stroked constantly, and a shining saber which he wore in a belt around his waist. It clanked loudly every step he took.

"What's going on?" he bellowed, and everyone trembled.

Just as the Jews feared the peasants, the peasants were in terror of Dmitri Avnesy. Within a few moments he put everything in order. His deputies broke up the crowd. The peasant put in his complaint and the Lipsches were taken into custody.

This wasn't the end of it, of course. Justice had to be done. And so as a result of this incident, I got to learn just how justice is achieved between Jews and Russians.

How? Well, the Jews held a meeting in the Bes Medresh where everything was discussed from every angle, and in addition a large amount of money was collected. Then a delegation of Jewish elders went to the authorities. That is to say, the constable, Dmitri Avensy, had the opportunity to display what a skillful arbitrator

* Plural of goy, or non-Jew.

he was, and how he could save the courts the trouble of trying a case.

He devised a brilliant compromise between the concerned parties: His plan was that he was to be bribed. The elders agreed to his plan because they felt that a Jew in the Russian courts would be "eaten alive." A trial had to be avoided at all costs.

It wasn't just the constable's palm that had to be greased. No! The incident gave an excuse to every Russian with a little bit of power to stretch out his hand to the Jews. The elders paid, and paid and paid. The hope was that all this money would seal the Russians' lips and the story would not be known beyond the town.

Other less significant precautions were taken as well. The merchants who dealt in grain were warned to be scrupulous, and the members of the Lipsche Company were told not to show their faces on the street for quite some time.

The following Sunday the peasants appeared at the market, friendlier than ever. My grandmother treated several to brandy and knishes. I did the serving. "You're a good Yid," one of them said to me. I wasn't *"Nash* David" anymore—maybe they could see it in my eyes.

One day I met Alter Richels on the street and he said, "Since I advised you to come here, I feel responsible for you. Would you like me to be your teacher? From now on come to my house on Thursday nights and bring my grandson Gur Aryeh and Shmuel Shocket."

I thanked him profusely, and could not wait for Thursday to arrive when we would fast and stay up all night studying. Each Thursday this was the custom in commemoration of our ancestors' temple, which had been destroyed by the Romans.

My friends and I were welcomed into a small study by Alter Richels. He opened a Gemara* and we began to read together. "What do you think this passage means?" he asked gently, and then listened to us with care and patience. His eyes would twinkle. "I'm learning so much from you boys." He drew us out on each

---

* A part of the Talmud, consisting of commentaries on the Mishnah.

subject until our dull, simple replies were transformed into brilliant insights. We swelled with pride. It never occurred to us how much help he had given.

Even Shmuel Shocket lost his usual timidity. We would shout out our answers, and often so would Alter Richels. He did not try to act like an important, dignified person but became a young boy again, like us. This wise man was higher than all the world, but he treated everyone as his equal.

How different he was from my early tutors who beat me every time I stumbled. For the first time, instead of always hanging my head in front of a teacher, I began to look up and have a glimpse of how beautiful Torah was. I had studied blindly before. Now a wise man guided me, but with such a light touch that I never even realized it. It felt more like a party than a school. I look back on those Thursdays as the times of the purest and most innocent joys of my youth.

Those evenings, where did I get my energy? I went to the Bes Medresh to work some more. People praised me for being so zealous, but I was only doing what was pleasurable to me.

One day, a well-known man, Rabbi Berinen, visited Shumsk and was impressed by the long hours I spent studying. He gave me a letter and said, "Use this if you ever want to study at yeshiva." It was as if he could see into my future.

It was Alter Richels who made me hunger for learning. It was an appetite I could not satiate and caused me as many pangs as my grandmother's terrible cooking. I am sure it was not Alter Richel's intention that I satisfy it in the way I did. Not only was I studying holy books, but I was eagerly devouring secular ones as well. During this period in Shumsk I developed tastes that I would never give up, and that would always be in conflict.

My grandmother decided she must tell my parents about the letter from Reb Berinen. We went to a scribe, who wrote a letter to them, addressed the envelope, and for his services received a considerable sum.

I thought about how profitable his position was, and since people were always complimenting me on my hand, I decided I too would like to be a scribe, and the sooner the better. In order to do this I had to perfect the way I wrote in Russian, so that I would be able to address envelopes and write letters in that language. I managed to get some Russian books and I took a fresh goose quill and practiced writing.

I did this at the Bes Medresh because I did not want my grandmother to know I had books that were not in *loshon koydesh**— and at the Bes Medresh I never took them out unless I was alone. Each day I found opportunities to write, and sometimes I put down my pen and just started reading.

I was discovered once doing this by one of the *kest kinder,* Simcha Godels, a short man with thick glasses and coarse yellow hair that grew straight up. He was about forty years of age, and his wife was childless. As a youth he had lived in a larger city with his widowed mother. His father-in-law was a distant relation who had offered a large dowry, and when Simcha Godels's mother insisted on the betrothal, he came to live in Shumsk. But he never seemed to belong. He kept apart from everyone and liked to dress himself up, and people complained privately that his clothes were inappropriate—not that they deviated in any important way, but somehow they were not Jewish-looking.

"Is it so wrong to read a Russian book?" he said, and looked me over from head to toe as if he had never noticed me before. "Come to my house this afternoon and we can discuss it." I was afraid he was going to expose my sin of taking such books into the Bes Medresh and I dared not refuse.

The rest of the morning I had time to examine my conscience. How could one study Torah so ardently and still act as I had? Unlike most Jews in Shumsk, I had known Russian well from the time I was a small child. I had lived in villages where my family were the only Jews, and to survive we had to speak in the same language as the peasants around us. Russian was as natural to me as Yiddish or Hebrew, and I never could bring myself to believe it was a sin to read it—even now.

When I arrived at Simcha Godels's I was not in a contrite mood.

* The "holy language," i.e., Hebrew.

I was astonished when he said to me, "From now on, if you want to study Russian, I want you to come to my house daily. I will give you as many Russian books as you want and study along with you."

Simcha's wealthy father-in-law had provided him with a private study. We spent the afternoon there at a table piled high with books. In addition to reading, I practiced penmanship. I did not have to look up every second to see if anyone was watching me. Time passed quickly, and I was completely absorbed.

I was startled when there was a knock on the door. Bella, Simcha's plump sister-in-law, came in bearing a tray of food. I could hardly believe the delicious feast that had been provided—onion rolls, pancakes, knishes, and a pitcher of warm milk. We cleared the table and Simcha and I shared this meal. I ate until I thought my stomach would burst, and later, when I went home to grandmother, my heart did not contract when I saw the dinner she served.

So it happened that I had a secret which I kept from all, and that is that I went to Simcha's house. I saw he really did not have much to teach me—I could teach him! But he encouraged me. Everything I mastered brought him joy. He even bought new books in the subjects that interested me, like mathematics. Even without his praise I would have worked hard, because some force was driving me on. No matter how much I read in the Bes Medresh or at Simcha's, I wanted more.

Simcha began to pour out his secret thoughts, talking to me as if I were an adult. He was miserable in Shumsk. He dreamed of a larger world. The enormous dowry had not been worth it. Over and over he warned me, "Don't let them trap you with an early marriage. That's the fatal step."

Slowly I began to see what his intentions for me were. Although it was too late for him to try—he was married and settled, and possibly never had the ability—his dream was that I would attend a Russian gymnasium, for, he believed, with such an education I could attain any position I desired. The study of secular subjects was the magic key to a world he had only a little better understanding of than myself.

Sometimes when I was struggling to balance an algebraic equation, I would notice he had closed his eyes, had sat back in his chair, and was humming a dance tune. I wondered what he was imagining. Perhaps a ball in a nobleman's house, or even at the czar's palace? A few moments passed and he snapped to attention.

"Are you working? That's good. Don't stop . . . don't lose a single moment."

I knew our session was over when I heard a knock on the door and then the clink of dishes on the tray Bella carried.

One day, I came home from a visit to Simcha Godels, stuffed with Bella's treats, and when I opened the door it was not my grandmother sitting in the chair, but my mother. I ran to her and began to kiss her. Then I noticed she was gazing at me with great sadness and I became frightened.

"What's wrong? Why did you come here?" I asked.

"You know better than I. Where have you been?" Her eyes were burning me.

"At the Bes Medresh," I faltered.

"At Simcha Godels's."

"How did you know?"

"A peddler was passing through Shumbar, and along with his merchandise he brought this news of how my son behaves. I came here immediately. My child, why did you have to stab my heart with such pain? Every day you visit with an unbeliever."

"That's not true," I protested.

She interrupted me with a scream, "To me he's a heretic!"

"But mother, all I did was learn to read and write Russian better, and I don't think it's a great sin. I think it's a benefit because it will enable me to make money."

"Look how he answers." She shuddered. "Look what little respect he shows. I'm afraid that now you've been completely corrupted." She gave me a look, as if I had been her enemy even when I was an infant in the cradle. I felt tears coming to my eyes.

"When I go to his house, his sister-in-law feeds me and I pack so much food into me that when I come home I don't have to eat up grandma's food." I realized my mistake to answer like this when I saw how pale my mother became. At first she could not talk at all; then her voice came out hoarse and low like a moan.

"Oh, my poor child . . . oh . . . oh . . . God have pity . . . my poor child. . . ."

She went to the wall and put her head against it.

By this time I was so frightened, I was weeping, and finally she took pity on me and put her arms around me.

"Poor child, don't you know they have hired a Russian kitchen maid? You have eaten *treyf!*"*

I started to gag. I didn't notice that my grandmother had arrived and had heard everything.

"It's my fault," grandmother said. "Why didn't I watch after him more closely? David, why did you eat there? Didn't you get enough here? Didn't you like what I cooked?"

What could I say? I assured her I liked her food. She sat down in a chair and was sobbing and blowing her nose. My mother was doing the same. Their eyes were all red; they kept beating their chests with their fists and looking up to the heavens for guidance.

"Promise you will never speak to Simcha Godels again," they demanded.

I hesitated, and this made them cry all the louder. I might have withstood one of them, but not both. In the end, I solemnly promised what they wanted.

Even this did not reassure my mother. The next day she left Shumsk, but when she parted from me there was a look of misery in her eyes. It was clear she wanted to stay in Shumsk to look after me herself, but it was impossible because my father's livelihood was at the mill in Shumbar.

I kept away from Simcha Godels's. He came looking for me at the Bes Medresh. To all his questions, I answered with a blank expression.

Maybe he guessed what had happened. He gave me a bitter smile. "So this is what comes of all our efforts. I just hope the lessons I gave you were not completely wasted."

* *Treyf:* Food that is not kosher.

* * *

My father's mill failed and there was nothing keeping him in Shumbar. Since my mother was so anxious to supervise me, she persuaded him to leave, telling him that he might as well be poor in Shumsk. They came one afternoon. There were no wagons of furniture and goods, since they no longer possessed anything. Everyone squeezed into Grandmother's house. She welcomed them warmly and did not resent such a large family moving into her two rooms. Grandmother was only glad that she could help and that we were all together.

To my parents she gave her bed and put a curtain up in front of it. The trunk that had been mine was good enough for her now. My sisters slept in the same room as my parents, and my brothers and I slept in the kitchen with my grandmother. I was sleeping on straw again, like in Shumbar.

My father had no work and was living off my grandmother. He decided to go to Vishnivets to Rabbi Joseph Radvilla to consult with him about whether he could ever make a decent livelihood. This rabbi was credited with performing great miracles, and people traveled far to wait in his courtyard for an interview. We were all anxious for father's return.

A week went by, and finally he came back. His expression was so sorrowful that he looked ten years older. His back and head were bent, and his walk seemed a bit crooked as he entered the house.

"*Nu*, what did he say?" my mother cried out, and tried to smile. She put aside the potatoes she was peeling.

"What did he say? If only he had said something."

"This is no time for riddles."

"I waited for five days to see him. There was a big bag and everyone put a piece of paper in it with their names. The rabbi's helpers drew out names at random, but mine was not selected. I saw already it was a bad sign.

"Finally I was called up. I went into the room where the rabbi was. He was drinking some tea and seemed to be in a good mood. I told him my problem, and as I spoke, his face and body looked as if they were turning to stone.

" 'When will I be able to support my family?' I asked.

"He stared into my eyes sadly and said, 'Silence is golden.'

"He would not utter another word. Two of his Hasidim came up to me and said, 'You'd better leave so others can talk to the rabbi. He won't speak while you are present.' "

My father added, "So now, my wife, you know what the future holds."

"If he said nothing, then it means nothing," my mother answered and continued peeling the potatoes.

That night when we children were supposed to be sleeping, I heard her pitiful sobbing in the next room.

After my father's trip to the rabbi, both my parents became resigned to their fate; they would have to struggle for every crust of bread. From day to day my father came upon small jobs he could do and earned a little money. My mother began to take in laundry. Piles of damp clothes were everywhere. The pressing was done at a narrow wooden table with a heated iron ball and a wood block. Hindah spent a whole day painstakingly pressing a ruffled dress and then hung it in the window to display her work. Every time I saw it, I felt sick thinking how she strained her eyes to make every pleat perfect. Shivah ran back and forth to the well in the back of the house for buckets of water. She was only eleven years old, and already her hands were red and callused.

It was a poor town and there was not enough money to be gotten from the laundry or from my father's errand running and his peddling. But my brothers and I were never permitted to help; we were to go to the Bes Medresh. My mother would not allow anything else. She was stern with us, always crying, "Study, study." Her ambitions for her sons, and particularly for me, were high. She was determined that I make a better life for myself. Perhaps I would even raise the whole family up.

It seems everyone had ambitions for me—my parents, Alter Richels, Simcha Godels—but I doubt if I would have gone anywhere had it not been for the death of Mordechai the Shochet.* If he had

---

* Person authorized to slaughter animals according to kosher requirements.

not died when he did, I probably would have stayed in Shumsk the rest of my life.

Mordechai left behind a fortune—in debts. This state of affairs was not his fault. The community should have examined its conscience for how poorly they rewarded a pious and scholarly man. A little more could have been eked out for his salary.

No one cared. Only when he died was there a fuss because now the housewives had to travel several versts, often on foot, for kosher meat. A replacement had to be found for the deceased.

It happened that Mordechai was survived by a wife, Bracha, and an only daughter, Perl, who was of marriageable age, and so it was decided that the best plan was to find a boy with ability and betroth him to the daughter. My parents were astonished when some of the town elders approached them and said they would like me to be the groom and consequently train to be a *shochet*. They refused without hesitation. Even the suggestion filled my mother with bitterness.

I was relieved at my parents' refusal. I was at an age when I was not particularly interested in girls. As a result of what had happened, I took special pains to take a long route to the Bes Medresh to avoid going by Perl's house. As for how the community would solve its problem, I did not know and did not care.

But it seems even this long route did not protect me. One day I heard someone calling, "David, David"; it was Perl. I had to stop on the street and see what she wanted. She rushed up to me and pressed a pair of eyeglasses into my hand.

"Here, bring these to my mother. She's praying and she forgot them at home."

Before I could object, she ran off and I was left with the eyeglasses. I was not happy about the errand, but I saw it would have to be performed. It occurred to me that my friend Shmuel might help me. He always did whatever I asked.

When I got to the Bes Medresh, I found him waiting. I said, "Shmuel, I have to deliver these glasses to Bracha. I want you to come to the women's section with me."

I was amazed when he answered rudely, "Do you expect me to go among the women looking for Bracha? I refuse."

I gave him an angry look that I hoped pierced him to the heart and then went immediately to the stairs leading to the women's section.

This was the first time I had ascended them. A worn curtain covered the door. I pulled it to one side and looked. All of the benches on this upper floor were full. I had heard that many of the women came every day before dawn and prayed until after one o'clock. Now I saw how it really was. Some of them sat in a trance. Others prayed and read psalms. Yet others shouted and screamed, and some who could not read just sat and shook.

Shmuel startled me by coming up from behind and tapping me on the shoulder. He was nearly crying and pleaded for forgiveness. "David, I'd do it for you if it was another woman, but not Bracha. Don't you know that since Mordechai died, they have been trying to marry Perl off? If I went in with the glasses, everyone would think the match had been concluded."

I flinched. But when Shmuel left me, I went inside to get it over. How could I escape? The women had stopped praying and were staring at me. My face was burning as I searched about. I found Bracha in the back of the room where she sat with her arms covering her head, crying bitterly and mourning her dead husband. I dropped the glasses into her lap. She looked up and tried to say something, but I ran away.

Two weeks later I was returning home, and this time it was not Perl but Bracha who stopped me on the street. She took my hand, telling me she wanted me to come to her house. I would have liked to run away, but I felt I had to be respectful and obedient. We made our way along the street slowly because Bracha was sick. She stopped frequently to rest and to regain her breath—and the whole way people stared.

We came to the house. It was dilapidated, slanted, and broken, with a big hole in the roof. Here, I thought, is found misery worse even than at my home. When Bracha invited me inside, I suddenly felt like bursting into tears. I felt afraid. Was I to live here? Was this my future? Bracha had to pull on my hand to get me through the door. Then I saw a gloomy room with a few broken chairs and a table. A pile of rags served as a bed.

Perl was stretched out on them and stared up through the hole in the roof. When she saw me she became upset. She started up and her skin, which was usually pale, became red. First she tried to cover a rip in the sleeve of her dress, and then gave up and covered her face with her hands instead. The girl was really pathetic, so small and thin that she seemed all bones. She had long red braids and looked about ten years old, even though she was fifteen.

"See, daughter, we have a guest. Come talk to him," Bracha said, and pushed her toward the table. Perl sat down and I did too. Then Bracha left us alone. We sat in silence and were both ashamed. At first I would not even look at her, just stared up at a cloud visible through the hole in the roof. It looked so white and plump, and I wished I were outside. Then I glimpsed Perl's face and noticed tears slowly sliding down her cheeks, one by one. She did not even trouble to wipe them away.

"What does your mother want?"

"I think she wants you to write a letter," she said in a voice that was no more than a whisper.

"Go . . . get her then," I ordered.

Just as she touched the door handle, her mother fell into the room, and Perl had to suffer this additional humiliation, that Bracha had been listening at the door.

Her mother demanded that she get the writing materials; apparently they had been made ready in advance. Perl set them before me with trembling hands, almost overturning the bottle of ink. Bracha began to dictate, and it went slowly because she cried the whole time.

This is the letter I wrote:

My dear brother-in-law:

I have no one to pour out the grief from my embittered heart. It is only because of you, it is true, since Mordechai died, that I receive two and one-half rubles a week, but nothing more. Today nearly the entire roof fell apart. When it rains the whole house is wet. A splinter of wood we don't have for the winter. My only daughter doesn't have a winter coat. Shortly the pension will stop. I don't like to talk to anyone about this. No one, not a single soul knows this. Anyway, my brother-in-law, only to you do I appeal and pour out the sorrow of my bitter heart.

Your sister-in-law,
Bracha

You might think I was made of stone, to see all this suffering and these appeals for help and to be able to withstand them. My conscience did prick me; I did squirm in my seat and think perhaps I should take up the burden. Yet, the first moment I could, I ran out. I was in such haste that I forgot to kiss the mezuzah* on the doorpost. Simcha Godels's words were ringing in my ears, not to tie myself down to an unsuitable wife—and so his lessons had not been completely wasted.

After this I never saw Perl. She worked lugging buckets of water or plucking chickens, and these jobs brought her through the streets of Shumsk. But she avoided me well, and we never even met by accident. But if, like me, she did not want the match, the town felt differently.

One afternoon when I arrived at the Bes Medresh, there was a stranger there, a *sheliach*† who was going around collecting to build a new temple. I introduced myself to him, and somehow our conversation gradually turned into an examination. People gathered around us, and soon it seemed as if nearly all the men in Shumsk were at the Bes Medresh to witness this—just as if a bride's family had hired an examiner to test me, as was customary before a betrothal. I was familiar with the passage in the Talmud upon which he questioned me and answered easily.

When he was finished, the *sheliach* said, "Call this boy's father."

There was a stir, and the *shammes* rushed out and came back after a while with my father. The *sheliach* was now standing at the pulpit, and when my father was brought before him, he addressed him as if giving a sermon.

---

* A small oblong container affixed to the front doorpost and containing a small scroll on which are printed verses from the Bible. The orthodox Jew touches his fingers to his lips and then to the mezuzah upon leaving and entering the house.

† Emissary.

"I want to tell you that your son is a rarity. He is stagnating here. Unless you send him to yeshiva, nothing can become of him. He should go to the one in Slonim in Lithuania, or better yet to the one in Kishinev in Bessarabia, and all that would be necessary would be a passport, a letter from the *rav*, and the usual expenses."

My father replied, "Two of the things you mention are easy. A passport costs two rubles, and a letter from the *rav*—for that one doesn't need any money at all. In fact, he already has a letter. But the expenses—where can I get them? Can a child travel naked? Can a fourteen-year-old boy walk to Kishinev?"

"There are ways of overcoming difficulty; it is no sin to appeal to a rich relative."

My father considered his words and said, "Perhaps you are right."

My friend Shmuel Shocket's older brother Isaac came forward. "If you weren't so stubborn, Harav Leibish, we would take this boy and we would pay for him to learn the laws of slaughtering. All we ask is that he be matched with Perl." An assenting murmur rose.

My father turned to him coldly. I saw the anger flash in his eyes that people had discussed the matter and connived behind his back in order to force him. He knew when he came home he would have to answer to my mother. If I became the Shumsk shochet she would never forgive him.

"If it is so urgent, why don't you teach your brother Shmuel? If only you had exerted as much effort to support Mordechai while he was living as you do to fill his position!"

The answer, to which all agreed, was "Shmuel is not capable. Your David is more proficient and would be better for the job— and someone has to serve in that capacity."

I felt frightened when I heard these words and slipped away. Simcha Godels was waiting for me in the small vestibule. There was a wild look in his eyes as he said, "My advice to you is to run away to America before they catch you. Don't let them ruin your life with this marriage. . . . There are probably more opportunities in America than to be gained by going to gymnasium. And if you go, maybe I will follow you!"

I ran away, but not to America. Instead, I ran home. Now that I think of it, I would have saved myself a lot of trouble if I had heeded his advice, but it seems I was not to go so directly to America; I had to make a more roundabout trip. His words would come back to me at a much later time, but now I rushed home, threw myself into my mother's arms, and poured out all my unhappiness.

She comforted me and I became calmer. Then suddenly both of us were alarmed at the sound of footsteps outside. It sounded as if a great many people were coming to our house. My mother peeked out the window and gasped. The rabbi's wife, Kayle, was leading a delegation of women to visit us.

"Quickly, my child," she cried, "hide in the next room."

Just as I withdrew, a loud knock was heard. I was crouching at the door and peering through a crack. My mother greeted the women in a decorous manner. "Please come in." There were about ten of them, all older and pious matrons whom my mother venerated. I saw how pale she became, how weak she suddenly looked. I felt I could not escape; there was pressure from all sides. In my misery I was chewing on my lip and it started to bleed. I wiped it on my sleeve, never taking my eyes from the crack.

Kayle, a small, dark woman with gold earrings, took my mother's hand and said, "Chaya Sarah, we will leave only after you have consented to a match as perfect as perfect can be."

The others crowded around my mother so that I could hardly see her.

"Chaya Sarah, please consent."

"Don't be stubborn, let us go home. Our families are waiting for us."

"Do you intend to defy the entire community?"

"We never thought you were so selfish."

"Look at her—how puffed with pride she is."

"Isn't the position good enough for your son?"

This went on for quite some time, until Kayle noticed that my mother was tottering and looked as if she would faint.

"Let her sit down. Leave her alone for now," she ordered.

The women cleared away from my mother, and a glass of water was brought to revive her. How dejected she looked, and I was certain she would concede. But when Kayle approached her, my mother grasped her arm and said in a pitiful voice, "How can I hurt my oldest daughter by allowing my son to marry first? Please don't make me bring shame on her."

The others began to object, but Kayle quickly quieted them. She considered my mother a long time, and finally said, "Don't torment this poor woman. We have no business here, and I won't deal with this matter anymore." She ushered the others out of the house.

That evening Kayle returned and talked for a long time with my parents. After she left I was told I was going to be sent to Proskurov. I had a rich aunt and uncle there who had a shop. They were not known for their generosity, but maybe if I showed up with my letter from Reb Berinen, they would be willing to send me to yeshiva. The *sheliach*'s words had given my father great hope that they would assist me. My mother, and particularly Kayle, saw it was best for me to leave so that shame would not be brought on Perl because of the refusal.

The night before my departure to Proskurov, I was restless. I went out for a walk. I am not certain why, but I wandered by Perl's house. I was thinking it was because of her I had to leave my family.

She was standing out front, still, her eyes closed, almost as if she were sleeping. I came up to her and greeted her. Her eyelids fluttered open. For a moment a look of panic went over her face, but then she recovered and said coldly: "Why did you come by here? Is it because you forgot to kiss the mezuzah on the doorpost?"

Then she turned and went inside.

⌇2

I learn to be independent

PROSKUROV, 1889 (SPRING AND SUMMER)

THE NEXT MORNING I left before dawn. It was March 1889. I was just fourteen years old, and I had been in Shumsk for a little less than a year. I was riding in a canvas-covered wagon, called a *fura* in Russian, with a troika of horses. There were ten people. A wooden bucket was attached to the rig and kept banging against the side. Only half the passengers were covered by the top, so if it started to rain, we who sat in front would get wet.

I was traveling with a group of women who were visiting the graves of their parents at the Mikolayev cemetery. Leibish, the coachman, had said he would take me along for free. At Mikolayev, one of the women, Chaya Shifra, was going to take me with her to her sister's for the night, so lodging would not cost me anything either. The only money my father gave me was a half ruble, because the next day I had to find a peasant to give me a lift from Mikolayev to Proskurov, and I would need something to tip him with.

When we set out, the coach was filled beyond capacity. The coachman let the horses run quickly and the women began to shout:

"My legs are getting squeezed."

"My soul is being jolted."

"We're going to crash!"

I sat crushed in among them but paid little attention. My thoughts were too occupied with reviewing how it had come about that once again I had to be separated from my parents. It was really my *tefillin* which had started me off on my journeys. If not for them, Alter Richels and his companions would never have come to the village. And it was because of Alter Richels that I went to Shumsk, and if I had never gone to Shumsk, I would never have met Perl, or had to set out for Proskurov. If only my great-grandfather knew what troubles his *tefillin* were causing me.

I wished none of it had happened. I was a year older since my bar mitzvah, but not any braver. It was terrifying to go to a strange city with only a half ruble in my pocket, and to go to relatives I had never met. What would they be like?

For a long time I held back my tears, but then they came in a torrent. The women noticed and all their attention turned to comforting me.

Mrs. Lipsche, with her not-too-pretty daughter, was sitting in the back of the wagon beneath the canopy. The daughter said, "With God's help you'll be a great man," and Mrs. Lipsche, who had recently taken up the habit of snuff, gave me a sympathetic look just before taking a long snort.

Chaya Shifra was sitting next to me. "What will your mother and grandmother say when they hear I let you cry like this? Aren't I responsible for you? Come, now. Surely there are other thoughts besides sad ones. Did you go to Kremenets last week for a passport?"

"Yes."

"Well, what did you see there?"

At this she roused me. "I saw Isaac Ber Levinsohn's house." This Jew was famous, and it had been thrilling to me to see where he had lived.

"So who is this Levinsohn?" she coaxed, probably only pretending not to know.

I was astonished at her ignorance and had to enlighten her. "Not only was Levinsohn a scholar, but he had great courage. Perhaps you heard how Jews in the city of Zuslov were arrested on false charges of ritual murder. Who was to come forward and defend them? Who dared to be their champion? Levinsohn. He could not rest until they were free. He wrote tracts on Jewish customs to show they were humane. To whom do you think he sent them? To the czar! And what was the czar's response? Were soldiers sent to arrest Levinsohn? No. The czar was so impressed that he began to correspond with this Jew."

A woman on the bench in front of me turned and said, "Would you like to hear how one of these letters saved him from evil?"

Forgetful of all my troubles, I nodded eagerly. She said, "One winter night an officer, who might have mistaken Levinsohn's house for a tavern, ran inside and began to shout for a brandy. He was quite drunk already and pushed past the servant into Levinsohn's study, where he screamed at Levinsohn, 'Show some respect and take off your yarmulke.' Instead of complying, Levinsohn calmly went to his chest and took out a letter with the czar's signature. Immediately the soldier became sober. He dropped to his knees and began to weep and said he would not leave unless he was forgiven."

Now that one story had been told, each woman had a tale. They opened packets of bread, cookies, and apples and shared them with me. We passed empty rolling fields that went on and on, and a few dark peasant huts. The sky was grayish and the whole world seemed uninhabited. The only signs of other humans were the wreaths which had been left at roadside shrines to the Virgin Mary. Then suddenly some small village would come into view. The first sight was of the wells with their high poles and crossbeams. The dogs rushed out and snarled at the *fura*. They were half-starved creatures with thin coats. One limped, another was half blind, still they barked ferociously. The peasants gave us sullen looks. We did not stop until we came to Lechoritz, a Jewish town, and there I prayed. Then we drove on to Mikolayev.

We arrived after nightfall in Mikolayev. Everyone went to an inn, except for Chaya Shifra and myself. We left the others and walked up a road of stones which was uneven and slanted like the bed of a dried-out river. We came to an old, brown wooden house with decorations around the windows. Chaya Shifra knocked on the door with the flat of her hand.

"Who is it?"

"You don't recognize Chaya Shifra, your own sister?"

"Yossel, go open the door so that my Chaya Shifra should be able to come in."

"Damn bitch, stop bothering me and go open the door yourself."

"I can't take my breast away from the child's mouth. *Nu,* Yossel, go already."

"You can go six feet under."

It was cold outside and Chaya Shifra and I were shivering. She said, "Let's go to the inn. There the door opens and we can go inside and warm ourselves." As we left, the sounds of crying and screaming followed us. Yossel and his wife were cursing each other. When we had gone a little further, we heard them cursing each other's parents, and when we were almost out of sight they had begun on their grandparents.

The inn was a small wooden building with a shed for horses and a henhouse nearby from which I could hear clucking; and it was a much sweeter sound than what my ears had just been treated to. Chaya Shifra threw open the door, and we went inside. We found a large room with a big stove of whitewashed bricks. People would sleep on benches and on the ledges. Meanwhile they were eating and drinking at a table with plates of stuffed cabbage, potatoes, bread, and a pitcher of kvass.* The only thing missing was a samovar, and soon the inkeeper, a short, fat man with a triple chin and bushy eyebrows, carried one in. It was a big yellow brass one, and I was grateful when Chaya Shifra put a glass of tea in my hand. She even managed to get me a cube of sugar to hold in my mouth while I sipped. When people asked me why we had come back to the inn, I tried to say as little as possible because I did not want to embarrass Chaya Shifra. A servant girl went outside and threw

* A Russian beer.

more logs into the stove opening, and the heat was really good. I felt safe and contented.

But this mood did not last long. Soon a disheveled woman with a ripped scarf on her head burst wildly into the room. She stood for a moment looking around, her bloated stomach bulging out and her mouth all sucked in because she had no teeth. Then she noticed Chaya Shifra and screamed, "Come, dear sister. Don't be insulted by my good-for-nothing husband. Come home with me."

Chaya Shifra tried to calm her. 'I'm not insulted, but you see I can't come. I have a boy I promised to look after."

The woman gave a terrible wail. "What boy? . . . Don't you care about your sister? Come!"

She grabbed her arm and started to tug with all her strength. "The boy will be all right. What about my children? They should have no mother if I leave this inn without you," she screeched. I was afraid she would start uttering some of the curses I had heard from the street.

Chaya Shifra tried to hold back, but it was no use—and maybe she had the same fear I did. She let herself be dragged from the inn, and gave me only a regretful look.

The door closed. The innkeeper wiped his forehead with his handkerchief. "That woman's husband is a notorious drunkard. Tonight more things will go on at that house than at a fair."

It was little comfort to me that I avoided that "fair." I saw I had no place to sleep. Leibish, the coachman, came up to me and said, "What are you thinking about, David? What the czar is going to have for breakfast tomorrow?"

I knew if I answered him I would start crying again.

"Come," he said, and took me by the hand and led me out to the shed. There I watched him scoop up armfuls of straw and put them in the coach.

"This will be a fine bed for you."

I crawled inside and immediately fell into a sound sleep. In the morning I was being pushed from side to side. It was Leibish trying to wake me. "Hurry, a peasant is leaving right this moment for Proskurov."

I jumped up and, without praying or eating, ran to where he told me. It was true the peasant was setting out. I had to run after his wagon a little to catch up, although it was not difficult because the nag that pulled it was old and broken-down and went slowly. The peasant agreed to take me.

We kept climbing up higher and higher into some mountains, and the horse had great difficulty. Every few moments it had to rest while the peasant screamed and cursed. Near the tops of the mountains there was not much greenery, but it looked beautiful because the sky was clear and blue. We came to a large lake, and on the other side was Proskurov, with its high buildings and spires. I had never seen anything like it.

The peasant, an extremely tall man with a shaved head and a drooping moustache, took me to the outskirts of the city where he had a mill. I tried to pay him.

"Hold on to your half ruble."

As I began to walk away he called, "Listen, Jew, if you can't find your uncle, come back here to me at the mill. You speak good Russian and I enjoy talking to you."

I waved to him and trudged on. Because of the lake, the ground was swampy and the mud came halfway up my boots. My heart was beating fast in anticipation. The outskirts of Proskurov were like the country; there were small cottages with chickens and ducks wandering about. I saw a horse with its front legs tied together so it would not go off.

Finally I came into the city.

The view across the lake had astonished me, but now I was even more in a dream. How huge, how vast everything looked. In Shumsk the highest houses had two stories, but here there were rows of stucco buildings that reached up four stories high. Yet these were not the largest buildings. There were churches with thin towers, and there was an enormous gray stone palace surrounded by thick walls.

I saw it from afar and walked toward it. As I approached, soldiers marched out of a gate and began to drill. They wore immaculate white jackets with epaulettes and gold buttons, white peakless hats, dark trousers, and knee-high boots. I thought I had never seen such handsome, vigorous men. Their leader called out orders and they moved in perfect unison, marching, turning, brandishing their swords. I had watched Hasidim dancing with enthusiasm and spirit, but they did so awkwardly and without grace. What I saw now was more like a dance, and I was entranced. All thoughts of my aunt and uncle left me. I had to stand and watch, and watch. Who knows how much time went by before a man came by and scared me off by saying, "What are you gaping at?"

Then I walked away, but not to my relatives. The crowds of people on the street carried me along, and I was too much in a daze to resist. So many new faces whirled past. Thousands lived here, maybe ten times as many as in Shumsk.

I kept saying to myself, "So this is a city."

I wandered from street to street, amazed at all the shops, at all the wares. In Shumsk there was one cobbler, and in Proskurov I passed three cobbler shops in a few streets. And so with the tailors. I passed a man selling some kind of fruit from a cart, and I wondered what it was—I had never seen oranges before. They had been imported from southern Romania.

Then I came to a boulevard, and there I saw something wonderful. Soldiers with healthy, ruddy faces were sitting in a circle playing music. There were violins, gleaming horns, silver flutes. Every eye was fixed on the conductor, who waved a silver baton.

I thought, why is it so fashionable among Jews to weasel their way out of the draft? One gives himself a rupture, one loosens all his teeth, another bends all his fingers, another develops scabs or by not sleeping becomes underweight. What fools! What idiots! Why deform oneself to avoid military service? I felt if it was possible for me to stand among the soldiers, I would have done it without asking permission of anyone.

Music had always had a powerful effect on me, and the marches and waltzes they played lifted me up in waves. I think if ever I had the courage to travel, to leave what was known and go to the unknown, it came from that first afternoon in Proskurov. The city stirred in me the longing to see what the wide world had to offer.

* * *

It was late in the afternoon, and for the first time I remembered I had not yet had any breakfast, and had missed dinner the night before too. My stomach felt cramped.

I stopped a woman and asked, "Where do the Jews live in this city?"

She explained carefully and I followed her directions. My old worries about what my relatives would be like returned. I knew little about them. The only thing I remembered being told was how my father's sister Bobbah came to be matched with Nuchem. My distinguished great-grandfather, Harav Mentchel, proposed the match, and Nuchem's father, Simcha Katz, agreed. Ordinarily a wealthy man does not consent to a daughter-in-law who is poor and whom he has never seen, but one cannot refuse an esteemed and holy man.

The only precaution taken was that Nuchem's mother went to Bobbah's grandfather, Harav Mentchel, and asked, "If there is some defect, please let it be known before the marriage."

The grandfather, who happened to be a tall and extremely ugly man, answered, "You want to know how the bride looks? You should know she has no blemishes. She is—God forbid—not blind, not crippled, not crooked, not deaf, and not mentally defective. She is—may she not come under the spell of the evil eye—healthy and strong. You ought to know her one problem is that in all ways she resembles me."

Nuchem's mother was so overjoyed to hear that the girl was not diseased that she looked the grandfather over and said, "Oh, then she's swarthy."

"Yes."

"Well, a black field grows bread."

I came to Alexander Street, where I saw only Jews. Because I was a stranger, people immediately approached me and asked what I wanted. I explained that I was looking for my relatives. An old man volunteered to be my guide. We walked a little ways and came to a four-story house. It had never occurred to me that my relatives would live in such a house as this, so high, with thick walls and a wide door. Such a house looked as if it would stand forever, whereas the houses in Shumsk were all falling apart.

The old man led me inside and called, "Bobbah." When no one came, he said, "Wait here, your aunt will appear soon," and went out. I was in a vestibule with a few chairs, but I was afraid to sit down. Yet standing was no better. The floor was made out of wood, not packed dirt as at home, and my boots had dried mud on them that might crumble off and make marks. Through a door I caught a glimpse of a beautiful sitting room, a sofa with thick pillows and fringes, golden framed mirrors on the walls, wooden stands with vases and several plants. There were silk cloths hung on the walls and flowered wallpaper. Everywhere I looked was something that filled me with wonder, and shortly I became even afraid to breathe for fear of what I would soil or break.

A mirror hanging in the vestibule showed me how ragged and out of place I looked, and as I was gazing in it a second face came into view which made me gasp. Trembling, I turned around and saw a tall, dark woman in a red *shaytl*. She stood with her chest thrust out, her hands held behind her back, and her expression was fierce.

I was too startled to say a word. For a few moments we stood examining each other. The woman wore a hat made of velvet flowers with ribbons that trailed down her back, a silk scarf with fringes over her shoulders, a full silk skirt, and a matching jacket in black with velvet cuffs and collar. A gold chain hung around her neck, and she wore diamond earrings and several rings.

As dazzled as I was by this finery, I quickly realized that this must be my aunt. Since she was my relative I was ready to embrace her, but because of her angry scowl I did not dare.

She was the first to speak. "What do you want here?" she said in an impatient tone, staring at my knapsack.

"Aunt, I am your brother Leibish Hershik's son."

This must have seemed impossible to her and so she asked, "And what are you peddling?"

I repeated that I was her nephew. "My father and mother send their greetings."

"But where are you traveling?"

"I've come to see you."

"What? My brother sent you here for a visit?"

"Yes, Aunt," I said humbly.

She started to pace up and down.

I said to her, "I haven't prayed yet. Is there some place I can say my prayers?"

She jabbed her finger in the direction of a door directly behind me. "Go, do it."

Quickly I unpacked my prayer bag from my knapsack and left her.

I entered a tiny place which must have been a linen closet and soon donned my *tefillin* and began to pray. When I finished, I hardly felt like coming out. Then I thought maybe I could beg Bobbah for a slice of bread, because by now I was truly famished.

Just at that moment I heard my aunt saying to someone in a loud voice, "Wait, you will see." The door was flung open and she squeezed in beside me, so that the two of us were crowded together between the shelves of sheets. In the doorway stood my uncle Nuchem, a slender man with smooth yellow hair parted in the center and a thin beard. He squinted and looked me over from afar.

My aunt lamented, "See, here he is, the uninvited guest. I'm supposed to succor everyone."

I said, "A peasant said I could stay with him at his mill. Should I leave?"

I think my aunt was ready to answer yes, but my uncle beckoned to her and spoke in this way: "It's no great tragedy. He can stay a little. Do you want it said that we kicked him out? Just treat him as any beggar who comes to the house."

With these words he went off to his study, and my aunt took my arm roughly and pulled me to a large kitchen with a low ceiling from which pots and pans hung. In one corner sat a servant in a long white apron and cap, plucking chickens. She was a pretty girl, about twenty years of age. In my aunt's presence she averted her face. My aunt gave no explanation as she grabbed the birds from her and dropped them in my lap.

I had to set to work. I was instructed to work quickly, not to leave a feather, and not to dare to rip the skin. I felt dizzy and my hands were trembling, but I would rather have bitten my lips off than complain. The servant, Rifka, said nothing, but I saw she was looking at me in a sympathetic way. Shortly my aunt came back to see my progress.

She found a slight rip and screamed, "Do you do this to spite me, or because you're a *golem?*"*

Then she went over to Rifka and began to criticize her also. When I finished the chickens, I had vegetables to slice and peel, and so I was busy every moment until finally the dinner was ready.

My aunt let me come into the dining room. To my eyes it was beautiful. Even the well-to-do in Shumsk, like the Lipsches, did not have such a room or set such a table with gleaming white cloth, matching china dishes, and silver. Not only that, but there were eight chairs around the table and each one was the same. To one side was a small table on which was set a tray of crystal bottles of liquor. Uncle Nuchem sat at the head with a linen napkin tucked in his collar, and Aunt Bobbah sat across from him.

"Sit down," my uncle said, pointing to a chair.

I sat on the edge. The meal consisted of smoked fish, borscht, chicken, marinated cabbage, fried potatoes, and sponge cake with cherry preserves. My aunt heaped food on my plate in a pile, so it was all mixed up. I took about four mouthfuls and then put down my fork. My stomach was too contracted to eat.

Aunt Bobbah noticed and said, "Why aren't you eating? Are you longing for the bits of bread from your knapsack?"

Apparently she had inspected my knapsack and found some bread my mother had put in without telling me. Bobbah had forgotten that when she was my age she had little better to eat.

I tried to eat a little more, but I was so weary that I dozed off right in the chair. When I opened my eyes, the dinner plates had been cleared away and there was another guest present—Nuchem's mother, who had the same thin face and blue eyes as her son. She and Bobbah were arguing.

* *Golem:* A clumsy person; a simpleton.

"Look, daughter-in-law, you know I never interfere in your business, but in this case I must make an exception. Don't you see the child's exhausted? Give him a bed and put him to sleep. Don't be heartless."

"Let me know pain if I know where to put him to sleep."

"Ten rooms in the house and you can't find a place for a child? If you don't want him, I'll take him home with me and have the maid make a bed for him in the *sukkah.*"*

"By me, he can also sleep in the *sukkah.*"

First she called the servant to take me out to the *sukkah,* but suddenly changed her mind. She would take me herself. She grabbed my arm as before and pulled me to a tiny, half-finished hut in the yard, near the outhouse. My aunt got some bedding and threw it in.

"Why didn't you tell me you were tired?"

Before I got a chance to really look at the room, she blew out the lamp. I undressed in darkness, then felt around with my hands for the blanket and stretched out.

I slept a few hours and woke up with stomach cramps. If I had been at home, I would only have had to cry out and my mother would have come to me, full of concern. She would warm tea for me, or maybe place a wet towel dusted with pepper on my stomach. Here I tossed about, terrified that Aunt Bobbah would find out I was sick and be even more angry. Finally I got up and crawled along in a pitch black darkness and banged on the walls until I found an open window.

I jumped out of it, landed on my knees, and bruised myself badly. I barely dragged myself over to the outhouse. Then it was hard to climb up and creep back in through the window. Wrapped in my blanket again, I tossed and turned.

Then I heard someone knocking on each door the way the *shammes* did in Shumsk, and so I dressed in the darkness and went out through the window again. Fortunately I saw a man going

---

* *Sukkah:* A booth or hut set up outdoors chiefly as a dining area during Sukkoth, the Festival of Tabernacles.

along the street, and he told me how to get to the Bes Medresh.

There was an iron gate with a Star of David on top. The vestibule had a red and white tiled floor with a brass spittoon in one corner. Inside I saw men wearing ankle-length *talaysim.** The building was quite large, and all around there were big marble pillars with inscribed plaques on them. In front was a dais beneath a leaded window. From the ceiling hung an oil lamp and several heavy, black, iron candelabra with unlit candles. The whole effect was gloomy but awesome.

I spotted a place in one corner where I could wash and went to do so. The towel hanging there looked as if a hundred hands must have been wiped on it already, and that was what I had to use to dry myself. Then I took a book of psalms and went over to where people were gathering and began to recite.

More men arrived and we began the services. I prayed as well as I could, but had to stop often because the pain I experienced became worse. I could barely resist lying down on the floor and holding my stomach.

An older man standing beside me saw how I was squirming. At the end of the services he said to me in a kind voice, "What is the matter with you?"

I told him, and he took my wrist to feel my pulse.

"Come, I will give you something to stop your pain," he said.

He never asked who I was, just took me out and up a narrow winding street to his house. There I sat in a chair with thick cushions while he drew some tea from a samovar and then went to a desk with many small drawers. He opened several, took some powders out, and mixed them into the tea. I drank from the cup, and shortly my cramps stopped and I felt a pleasant heat spreading over my body.

"Would you like some more?"

In the second cup he put something else. I sipped it slowly and as I did, I realized I no longer felt anxious or worried about anything. It was like a dream, sitting in that room with its dark brown walls and dark furniture, and having this man beside me with his

---

* Plural of *tallis*, or prayer shawl.

long silvery hair and beard and his penetrating blue eyes. The more I drank, the happier I felt. We talked little and yet there was something calming about the man's presence; to me he was like the Angel Raphael, the healer.

When I finished the second cup he said, "You are well now, aren't you?"

I nodded.

"If you ever feel sick again, come to me."

I rose and took his hand. "May God refresh you, as you have refreshed me."

I went out into the street. Without hesitation I went to the Bes Medresh and prayed with exultation and faith that I would be protected from all evil. Then I returned to my aunt and uncle.

Bobbah was waiting in the hall for me.

"I hear you went to Israel the healer. Did you come here to Proskurov just to blacken my name? I don't need anyone to take pity on you. I will be maligned. Why didn't you tell *me* you have cramps? *I* would have done something instead of letting strangers take pity on you. At least you have shown what a sly person you are. My husband says you are to have a meal here—but then you must go!"

I sat down at the table with my head down. The food was served.

My uncle was biting into a spoonful of boiled egg when he said, "Why is it they sent you here?"

I said simply, "They thought you would pay for me to go to yeshiva."

I heard a crashing sound. My aunt was so shocked that she had upset her glass. My uncle was calmer. He smiled and drawled, "Did you know that those who are sent to study at yeshiva are supposed to be capable?"

"I have a letter from the son-in-law of the Benderer rabbi about my abilities," and for my aunt's benefit because she had called me sly, I added, "and my character."

When Nuchem heard this, he looked a little uncomfortable and demanded to see the letter. His way of addressing me altered, and he even thought to say "please" when he made his request.

I went to the *sukkah* and brought back Reb Berinen's letter. After reading it several times, my uncle passed it to my aunt with a significant look.

He cleared his throat. "After the High Holy Days, I'll send you to yeshiva," he said to me, and to my aunt, "With this letter he could be received anywhere in Proskurov. Put it away so he won't lose it."

I watched Aunt Bobbah fold it several times and put it in her pocket. I had not read it, but I understood that it extolled me— and also that I had just lost it.

Later I tried to understand why they had taken it away from me, and finally decided it was because my uncle was afraid that if someone saw the letter, I would not have to come to him for anything anymore.

On this same day, my uncle informed me that I would have to earn my bread while I was living with them, and he took me to his shop and put me to work. Nuchem sold merchandise to the shopkeepers from all the surrounding towns. There was a large room on the first floor for the customers, but I went to the cellar to join the apprentices who assembled packing cartons for the goods. There were three of us, with a foreman supervising, and I was given boards, paste, and a knitting spigot with which to lace boxes. It was at my uncle's shop that I learned endurance and to work long and hard. The cellar was always cold and damp, and I pitied the other boys, who were even younger than myself. We bent our backs over this work so many hours that when at last we were finished, we could hardly stand straight.

My only consolation was that in a few months the High Holy Days would come, and with them my release.

What it was like with my relatives, you can imagine. Every time I came in, I received Aunt Bobbah's sarcastic *"Baruch haba."** She and Nuchem hardly looked at me except when I had to eat, and I had little appetite. They kept asking me, wasn't I hungry? It was not for food I was hungry.

* Blessed is your arrival.

I tried to win their affection, but it was impossible. Nuchem ignored me, and Bobbah twisted everything I said or did into something that exposed my evil intentions. To her I was capable of every crime, even theft.

Once I delivered some packages for my uncle and received a tip from the customer. When I came in the house with the coins jingling in my pocket, Aunt Bobbah noticed and screamed, "What? Are you stealing from the shop now?" It hurt me so much to be called a thief that I took the money and put it on the table before her, and decided not to accept tips again. But whatever I did was wrong. Later Bobbah called me a fool for not saving up tips and buying some new clothes for myself. She said I went around in a ragged suit on purpose, in order to get sick and shame her.

Sometimes my uncle entered in the middle of one of these lectures. He immediately buried his head in a book or went out of the room. Maybe he was afraid he would feel a flicker of sympathy.

People told me he had been a kind person, but years of living with my aunt had hardened him. And why did he stay with her? Even with the pearls and laces, the satin gown and the plush cloak Aunt Bobbah wore when she went out, she was not much to look at. I heard it said that Bobbah was my uncle's good luck. The reasoning was that fortune had to take pity on a man afflicted with such a wife and make him prosper; if he divorced her, immediately calamities would beset him.

At home and at my uncle's shop I was unhappy, but elsewhere I enjoyed myself. The city was exciting to me. If I had had the time, I would have wandered about Proskurov's streets endlessly. For this reason I was always hoping my uncle would use me as a delivery boy. He loaded packages on my back that would have strained a grown man, but I did not care, because it gave me a chance to escape the shop. Coming back, I was free of my burden and could stroll along.

I had started to reflect on my life in a way I never had before. I remembered how I cried when I left the village of Shumbar and the peasant life I had known. It seemed to me I was making an important break from my family and starting to become a man. The truth was that my grandmother had fussed over me more than my own mother, and Alter Richels was always there to help and advise like a father. Then later my real parents came and joined me. Only in Proskurov was I really learning how to stand on my own. How lonely it was for me in my uncle and aunt's household. To whom could I turn? My heart bled, but I walked on the street with a smile and behaved cheerfully to everyone I met. When I had lived with my parents and been poor, I had not really suffered. Now, how strange, I was living with rich people, learning what true suffering was all about.

Well, why be sad all the time? Maybe the experience was strengthening me. I was learning how to judge people. I was learning to rely on myself to keep my spirits up. I was learning to work, and my body was getting stronger. All kinds of thoughts were flying through my head. Wouldn't it be nice to be rich? Then I would be independent and no one could treat me badly. Ambitions were taking hold of me, and I did not realize that some of them would not really be good for me. I would suffer later because of them.

Once I was passing through the central square, and all around me I saw windows, walls, and carriages draped in black. More and more people began to gather, and I got sucked into the center of the crowd.

I asked a man beside me, "What's the matter?"

"A general of the Orthodox faith has died."

Then he told me the name and I knew who it was. Every Jew had heard of this general because recently he had contributed new books and covers to the *shul** and no one could understand why.

In a little while the entire square was crowded with people, packed together so tight that not even a needle could have fallen to the ground. All waited to see the body. The procession was led by squadrons of soldiers who carried the casket, and following behind were four elderly Russian priests with forked beards, wearing long black gowns and high headdresses. They walked slowly by but suddenly came to a halt.

---

* Synagogue.

Several Jews in the crowd became nervous and took off their caps to show respect. Immediately the commander ordered that all hats be kept on, and as he did so, his soldiers lowered their rifles and went about picking out Jews and making sure the order was obeyed. I stood there trembling with fear and wondering what would happen.

Then I noticed a soldier on horseback leading a *hazzan**° dressed in a long white gown and wearing a *tallis,*† and along with him came his choir. They made their way through the crowd until they came up beside the casket. The same man who had offered me an explanation before whispered in my ear, "It seems the general is afraid to go to his final resting place without a *hazzan* and a choir performing over him."

On this afternoon, I saw the greatness of my people. It was like a theater. The *hazzan* waited until there was silence. In that whole sea of people, there was not a sound—and then suddenly he began to wail in a deep, low voice, the choir accompanying him. He sang with such feeling that it seemed like Yom Kippur. Through my own tears, I saw other Jews sobbing and wringing their hands. They closed their eyes, swayed back and forth, and forgot where they were.

When the *hazzan* was done, the commander gave a signal and once again the procession moved slowly toward the train station. The body was to be transported to Petersburg.

I returned to my uncle's shop to take up my knitting spigot.

I had little time for education in Proskurov, and this pained me. Not only was my knowledge not growing, but I was afraid I would forget what I knew and that when I entered yeshiva I would be shamed before everyone. I did not realize that the treasures Alter Richels had given me would never spoil. My knowledge and my sweetest childhood memories were one and the same, and one never forgets even the most minute detail of such a childhood. The Torah was woven together with caresses in my memory.

° Cantor.
† Prayer shawl.

Still, I did not understand this at the time, and I was constantly worrying. Whenever I could get away, I ran to the Bes Medresh. I tried to study there, but my mood was low, and I did not accomplish much. It was more tempting to mingle with people and receive the attention and friendliness that were lacking at home. Even if I did not say a word, I found it pleasant to stand on the edge of a group and listen to what others had to say. No one glared at me; no one hated me or bore me a grudge for every breath of air I took.

I met a variety of people, among them several who were planning on going to America, just as Simcha Godels had suggested to me. I listened to their talk and was fascinated by the tales of a land where the streets were said to be paved with gold. Some truly believed this, while others were skeptical. Those who were going to America were real "converts" ready to baptize others. All their conversation was of "a new life" and "opportunity."

I had no understanding of these people. To me it was bad enough that I was so far away from my family—it was horrifying to think of going halfway around the world. Little did I realize that all this talk of America was a net being thrown out wider and wider and someday it would pull in thousands upon thousands, including myself. Now only people who were a little strange, like Simcha Godels, talked and dreamed about it. In a few years it would seem as if everyone was leaving Russia.

I enjoyed the conversations I had at the Bes Medresh, but more important were the morning and evening services. The same *hazzan* who had sung at the general's funeral led the prayers. When I listened to him sing, I felt it with all my soul. It no longer mattered that Aunt Bobbah had scolded me or that Uncle Nuchem had been ill-tempered at the shop.

Effortlessly I memorized everything the *hazzan* sang, and also his mannerisms. The prayer melodies were always running through my head.

One time some young men at the Bes Medresh heard me singing softly to myself while I read Torah. They came over and asked me to sing aloud. I felt shy, but they acted in such a friendly way that

I complied. Then they insisted I let them take me to the *hazzan*. For him too I had to perform. The other men were pleased that I had learned an intricate melody, but the *hazzan* scrutinized me more carefully. First I had to go over certain parts several times, and then he began to sing and I had to repeat whatever he sang in exactly the same way.

Finally he smiled and said, "I only hope you'll sing this well at services."

He said I sang better than his own reader and I was to be given solos and would accompany him. He wanted me to come to him each afternoon to study and review the music.

None of this came about; the reason was that my relatives refused to buy a new suit for me. I could not appear in front of the congregation in my present outfit. My suit was too tight and the material so frayed that people could see through it. My boots had mouths so wide that they drank water. The *hazzan* happened to tell my aunt and uncle that if I had been five years younger I would have become a renowned singer, but now my voice would change in about a year.

Uncle Nuchem's response was "If that's the case, then a suit is not a good investment."

When the *hazzan* offered to pay for it himself, my relatives became infuriated.

A few weeks after this, I had to deliver a package to a cobbler. I arrived at his shop just after he had sold a new pair of boots to a soldier. The old ones were left on the counter—cracked, with run-down heels, but without holes. The cobbler said, "Listen, David, I don't want trouble with your uncle and especially not with your aunt. Let's trade this pair of boots left here for yours. Try them on. I'd like to dress you up completely, but let's start with the boots and see how it works out."

I tried to refuse, but he urged me, "Why don't you just see if they fit? You don't have to take them." While he talked, he took out some polish and started to shine the boots, and the leather took on a warm brown color. I began to think how pleasant it would be to have dry feet, and I could not resist just trying them on. I sat on a stool and pulled off my old boots, and the cobbler brought the new ones over to me. They fitted perfectly. If a boy can be said to be in love with a pair of boots, then I was in love with those. Still I hesitated. I felt they would get me in trouble with my aunt. I walked around the shop a few times just to enjoy them a little longer, and then I sat back on the stool and started to pull them off. The cobbler said, *"Nah*, David, keep them." With that little encouragement, I could no longer resist. I left the shop wearing my new boots, and everywhere I walked I had great pleasure.

But if I had known the scene that awaited me with Aunt Bobbah, I would have walked down to the lake at the edge of the city and thrown the boots into the water. Better to be rid of them than have to endure the insults she heaped on me, the screaming, the accusations, the enumeration of all my faults, the slap in the face I got when I said, "What does it hurt you if I have a pair of boots that don't leak?"

It happens my aunt was in the same tiny closet I said my prayers in on my first day in Proskurov, when I passed by, and she saw the boots for the first time. She gave a shriek and then pulled me inside. For more than an hour I had to stand there crushed against the wall and hardly breathing while she sermonized on all the trouble I caused her. My only hope was that she would turn around for a little while so I could put my hands over my ears, but I did not have such good fortune.

It was thus that I learned patience—to listen, to say nothing, and not to show on my face what I felt. These were skills I would need later on. In all my life, I never knew a person with my aunt's venom, but I met those who came close, and with whom I had to live and work. But at the time, I could hardly appreciate this valuable lesson, forced as I was to listen to my aunt sermonize until she was completely exhausted.

When she finally released me, it was with these words: "Take those boots back to the cobbler and get your old ones, or you'll go about barefoot from now on."

She had to go out, and we left the house at the same time. She was wearing a new sable coat. I noticed in Proskurov that the richer people were, the more fur they wore. One had a rabbit collar; another trimmed his boots. My aunt and uncle draped themselves completely.

My aunt got into a hansom cab. I walked quickly away, and the only thing I could think about was that as soon as I returned home, she would resume lecturing on the same subject. I kept blaming myself that I had been so foolish to take the boots. As I went down the steps to the cobbler's, they were already in my hand. Without a word I handed them to him. He needed no explanation; he could see how red my eyes were. He went to the back where he had thrown my old boots in a garbage bin.

While he was rummaging about for them, I overheard him saying to his wife, "May God shield me. It's not enough that the Almighty God took luck away from the Jews, but he also took away their intelligence. With a child like this one, they could be brought truly high."

That night I asked Uncle Nuchem to give me pen, ink, and paper so I could write a letter to my parents. I waited patiently for him to leave me alone because I wanted to pour out all my troubles. Soon I realized that my uncle was going to stay by my side and watch every word I set down. There would be no crying to my mother and father. All I wrote was this: "I hope if you want to send my brothers to yeshiva, that you will be able to afford to send them yourselves."

The letter was sent out, but I received no response.

The High Holy Days arrived. I went to services at Rosh Hashanah and then on Yom Kippur, when everyone fasted. In the *shul* candles were lit in a large casket for the dead, and soul candles were lit for the living; people trembled lest their candle be extinguished. Everyone made vows, wept, and prayed.

That evening my uncle took me to the home of a Zinkover Hasid. Many Hasidim were gathered around a table set with platters of gefilte fish, roast chicken, potatoes, sweetened carrots, and other delicacies, the odors of which rose like incense. The congregants made a toast to end the long fast, and what we ate tasted like a feast from heaven.

I was asked to sing. The host remarked that he loved a young boy's voice better than any other, and once I started singing he would not let me stop. The Hasidim surrounded me with ecstatic faces and shining eyes. Their bodies seemed to swell and they were uplifted to such a zealous mood that they all grabbed hold of one another and started dancing. I too danced and shared in their rejoicing.

After fasting and the moving experience of the Yom Kippur service, I was able to release all my feelings. I danced wildly, jumping high, kicking in the air, almost like a cossack. Others stopped to watch as I whirled round and round. My eyes were closed and yet I had some sense of where the others stood, and the furniture. Anyway, if I bumped into something, I did not feel it. I hummed the melodies and improvised my own tunes, which those who were musical took up and sang along with me. Completely in another world, I kept dancing faster and could have gone on and on. Finally my uncle started to shake me.

"David, we have to go home."

For a moment I didn't recognize him, but then I came back to reality.

"*Gut yontif,** Uncle," I said, and embraced him triumphantly.

We went out into the dark night and walked along the cobblestone street. I whistled a tune.

"Why are you so happy, nephew?"

"Because within the week I set out for yeshiva."

He said, "Listen, David, I see that you are no dreamer. Yeshiva is not for you. So you study? What does that matter? What importance can that have? That you get a reputation? Until you gain a reputation, you don't even have enough to travel back home. Start as an apprentice at the shop, and soon you'll work yourself up to being a gentleman."

I protested, "It's not to be one of your apprentices that my parents sent me here."

My uncle saw how upset I was and tried to calm me. "I'm not saying I won't send you to yeshiva. Just think about my proposal."

Despite his reassurance, I knew now that I could put little faith

---

* Happy holiday.

in his promises. Suddenly even the stars in the sky seemed dull and lifeless.

It was with a letter that I found release from my suffering. One day my aunt and uncle called me in to their sitting room. Uncle Nuchem searched in the pocket of his jacket and pulled out a crumpled letter.

"Here, for you . . ."

He threw it at me. I saw he had already opened it even though he knew the Talmud forbids reading someone else's mail. I carefully unfolded the sheet, and when I saw that the first line was "My dear son" and that it was from my father, my hands began to tremble.

The entire time I read, my aunt kept talking to Uncle Nuchem: "He's not getting any money here . . . and not only that, but tomorrow the train leaves Proskurov, and he will be on it. . . . You know something, he would be better off an orphan. Then at least people would pity him. . . ."

My aunt's words were upsetting enough, but what I read in the letter was more so. At first I felt hopeful, because it seemed my father had learned of my situation and was disgusted at how I had been treated. He wanted me to leave Proskurov as soon as possible. Then I learned the new plans he had for my future. My parents were still determined that I go to yeshiva—and now, under any conditions. They went to Perl's uncle and arranged that he should pay for me to go to yeshiva in Kishinev, and at the same time they had me betrothed to Perl. Later I would take over the position left vacant by Mordechai, the deceased *shochet* of Shumsk.

For a long time I had to listen to my aunt's opinions on this subject. She also told me that I was going to receive only three rubles toward my fare to Kishinev. With that I could buy a ticket which would take me two stops, and the rest of the trip I could push myself under the seats and hide when the conductor came around. I did not like to do anything dishonest, and more than that I was afraid I would be arrested. I pleaded with Bobbah to give me the full fare, but she was adamant.

Finally I was allowed to go to my room, and I stayed there the rest of the afternoon. I did not even come out for dinner, and no one came to inquire after me. Before I went to bed Uncle Nuchem came into the room quietly and said in a whisper, *"Nu,* here you have five rubles and have a safe trip." I pressed his hand and thanked him gratefully. "Stay well and stay rich," I told him.

That night I slept poorly. A story I had heard about a peddler woman kept running through my mind. This woman stopped in the town of Kiniv in order to nurse her ailing infant. Finally one day, Yakov, the treasurer of the *Hevra Kaddisha,* * was called. He put a feather under the child's nose, and when it did not move he declared her dead and prepared to take the corpse to the cemetery. He carried her away still in the cradle, which was a slatted one with ropes in four corners which were suspended from a ring. Yakov held the ring as if he were carrying a bird cage. He walked through a thick forest where it was cold and the ground was slippery. It happens his house was on the way, so he decided he would rest there awhile. Outside was a pile of cut logs on which he left the cradle while he went in and refreshed himself with tea. When finally he was ready, not only had it become dark, but a thick fog had settled over everything. He decided that it was dangerous to go out in such conditions and that he would leave the child and bury her the next morning. The following day he dressed warmly and set out to do his task. How astonished he was when he came and discovered the child on the woodpile, half frozen and crying.

All night I had disturbing dreams in which I was the child on the woodpile struggling to free myself.

I got up at daybreak in a restless and sad mood. At services I had a lonely feeling of being apart from everyone. I said good-bye to a few people, then went home. In my room I spread everything I owned out on my bed. The only extra clothing I had was a second *tallis katan.*† I checked its *tzizzis*‡ to make sure there were the required number, and then carefully folded it. My other possessions

---

* Burial Society.

† A short, jacketlike fringed garment worn under a coat or vest.

‡ Biblically prescribed fringes worn at the corners of the prayer shawl (*tallis*) and the *tallis katan* as a reminder of one's duty to the laws of the Torah.

were my passport, my prayer book, a book of musical rhythms the cantor had given me, my *tallis*, and my *tefillin*. As I was packing, my aunt put her head in the door and said, "Don't try and steal anything." Later, when I was ready to go and called to her, she would not come. I had to leave the house without a word to anyone.

I walked down the street a little ways when suddenly I heard someone call my name. It was the servant Rifka who came after me. I wondered, had I left something behind? Then I became alarmed because I realized it was more likely that something was missing and they thought I had taken it.

Rifka came up to me breathlessly. "Here, David, you will travel over thirty hours and I have packed you some food. You are only a child of fourteen. It is shameful no one gave you anything." Then she pressed something else into my hand and I saw it was the letter from Reb Berinen.

I said, "I wish you eternal life for your kindness."

"Dear child, I had better go or your aunt will miss me."

I threw my arms about her and hugged her hard, and then we parted.

I travel to Kishinev

ON THE ROAD, 1889 (Autumn)

I WENT TO the terminal, a big, square, stucco building with turrets, arches, and flags on top. Inside was a huge hall with a big clock on the wall and benches. I joined the lines of people waiting at the ticket windows. Now I carried Reb Berinen's letter, as well as food for my journey and what I believed was enough money to take me to Kishinev. My situation was not perfect, but the slight improvement made me cheerful, which shows how little it takes to lift a person up.

I was mistaken about the fare. At the counter the stationmaster said that a ticket to Kishinev was seven and a half rubles. I walked away from him in a daze. To have had hope a few minutes before was the worst thing for me, for now I was more crushed than I had ever been in my life. My only thought was that under no circumstances would I return to my aunt and uncle—but I had nowhere else to go. I wandered about the terminal.

People's faces seemed blank and unfeeling, and their voices echoed in a meaningless way in my head. Every heart, I believed, was as hard as my aunt's. It would be foolish to appeal for assistance. I would stay in the terminal until I became sick. And after that? I did not care. Poor people's lives were hardly worth living.

For a long time I wandered about until I was distracted by a raucous laugh that rose above the hum of voices. It sounded familiar to me, reminded me of a Jew in Shumbar called Mendel. Imagine my astonishment when I looked about and found this Mendel himself. He was a dashing, handsome Jew, swarthy and with a black moustache. It was said that women found him attractive and that besides his poor wife, he had several girlfriends as well. Along his jaw was a long, red scar, a testimony to his carousing and brawling.

In Shumbar my father had done business with Mendel's father, but had nothing to do with Mendel, and neither had I. But today, with all my problems, I did not feel particularly superior to him.

I greeted him heartily and received a warm response.

"What are you doing here, David?"

"It's not a pretty story."

"Then I'll really enjoy it."

I told him all that had happened, and immediately he said, "If my partner agrees, why don't you come along with us? We are traveling to the Meczibizer fair with some horses and we could take you as far as Razdiolny. From there you'll take the train to Kishinev and even have a ruble left over."

The result was that a few hours later I was squeezed between Mendel and his partner, Itze, on the bench on a wagon. Two black horses were hitched to the front, and behind were tied ten other animals they were transporting. We left the city. The noise of so many horses' hooves against the cobblestones was great. People stared with amazement as Mendel whipped the horses. In the countryside the road was rutted and we went more slowly. The two partners talked freely as if I were not present.

Mendel said, "My mother died last month. But don't be sad for me; it gives me so much pleasure that my father no longer has a wife."

I was shocked by such conversation and decided the best thing was to not pay attention. The only comfort I could find was that at least these two were not hypocrites who hid their evil behind silks and furs like my relatives in Proskurov.

We had gotten a late start, and soon the sky was gray and it was dark on the horizon. With difficulty we descended from a mountainous place, then through a burned-out forest. It was an eerie sight to see all the black trunks and their stumps of branches.

It was night when we came to a small village. On its outskirts a strange incident occurred. Just as we were passing the cemetery's wooden fence, the horses stopped and refused to move.

Mendel cursed under his breath and started to whip them. They walked backward a few steps and snorted.

"Get down," Mendel ordered us. My legs were like wooden sticks. There was no moon, only blackness around us, and I was afraid to take a single step.

"Do you see?" Itze said in a barely audible voice.

Mendel gave a low whistle.

I looked and looked, and then I saw something white flickering in front of me. It moved to one side, and then another white form started to move. My heart was pounding like a hammer.

"Quick, let's run away."

Mendel's hand tightened around my wrist. "You want they should chase us? Just stand still!"

Something brushed my face. Perhaps it was only the wind, but it felt like cold hands. We stood there a long time. The only thing that happened was that we began to freeze. Mendel ran forward and his whip streaked through the air like lightning. Suddenly he started to laugh.

"Fools," he screamed at Itze and me. "The housewife washed her clothes and hung them to dry on the cemetery fence. The shirts froze and the wind blew them onto the road."

We gathered the shirts and threw them over the fence so the horses would not be afraid. Then we climbed into the wagon.

We rode into the village and entered the courtyard of an inn. It was a one-story, thatched-roof building with a heavy wooden door. Inside was a large room with peeling yellow paper on the walls and a low ceiling. There were several wooden tables with people crowded around them. Everything was a confusion of brightness, heat, clattering dishes, strange faces, and strong odors.

Itze and Mendel went off to get themselves some food and forgot about me. The mistress of the inn approached me and asked to see my passport, and she wrote my name in a red book. This book was sent to the police daily, as everyone had to register with the authorities when staying somewhere overnight. Particularly there was concern that a Jew might try to travel somewhere illegally, and even in a small village like this there were raids of the inn in the middle of the night, when people were pulled out of bed and every corner was searched.

"Look how this child is shivering," the mistress said and shook her head. "Bring blankets and a warm drink," she called to a pretty girl of about twelve years.

"But I don't have money to pay for such things."

"Don't worry, my child. In this inn all are welcome. The rich pay a little more, and the poor pay nothing. In this way I never commit the sin of turning anyone away."

Soon I was wrapped in a quilt and eating heartily. After finishing my meal, I joined several guests who sat near the stove telling stories. I felt restored not just by the food and warmth, but by the kindness I had received that day. A heaviness crept over me and soon I was asleep.

When I awoke, the mistress was leaning over me and shaking my arm gently. "Stay up a little while, dear child. We are having a celebration. As soon as it is over, you will have a comfortable bed." When I heard these words, I became completely alert.

In a while I watched the mistress leading a thin old man who leaned heavily on her arm into the room. They had to stop frequently, but at last they came to a chair. The old man sat down with an air of dignity, and the mistress announced to her guests, "My father would like to tell you something."

The old man stroked his beard, smiled, and began to speak in a voice that I had not expected to be so deep and strong. "My daughter is going to bring some brandy, and you are all to help yourself. Today I am celebrating a *yahrzeit.**

"A year ago someone died, but truly it is not so much for that I

---

* The anniversary of someone's death.

am treating you, but because I want you to know how great my rebbe is. Now, to describe his greatness is going to take a long time, so please be sure you have enough to drink, and make yourselves comfortable."

A few people rearranged themselves in their chairs so they were reclining, a mother opened her blouse to nurse her infant, another woman took out some knitting and in various ways, each one of us settled down to hear the story.

My guests:

This inn where you are going to spend the night has been in my family for three generations—and this whole time, no traveler has ever been turned away. One has some money in his pocket, another has none; it never mattered. This was true since my grandfather bought the inn from the count. When my grandfather passed away, my father inherited it. Then I too received the deed. But what is a piece of paper worth? You will soon hear.

A little more than a year ago, the present count (this is, you understand, the grandson of the old one) decided he was going to sell his estate. He was a drinker, a gambler, had a lot of debts. What's the difference? In the end I had a new neighbor. A Russian general moved into the big manor near this inn. He brought with him his family, servants, and all his belongings. When he saw how difficult it was to manage everything, he hired a "minister of affairs," a Jew named Heschel Goldfarb. Such a Jew I hope I never set eyes on again, a man who was ready to cut someone's throat for the enjoyment of it. God forbid, not with a knife because that would be arduous physical labor. No, this one used his tongue, because it didn't make him sweat. His greatest pleasure was to bury another Jew. Immediately he noticed the inn; it was a nice place and I was earning a nice living, so he suggested to the general that maybe he should take it over. After all, why not? As a result I received a letter from the general written in this gracious style:

> I could get more for the inn, but since you are here so long I will let you stay for only two hundred rubles. I am giving you thirty days to sign a contract, but only for one year.

Now, you can imagine, such a letter one reads a few times over. I tried to decide what to do.

If my old rebbe was alive he'd have given me advice. After he died I went to see his son out of respect, but when the son died and the grandson took over, I just sent over a few rubles and that was enough. I am an old man, so how could I consult with such a young person? I thought and thought about my situation and realized that it could not be worse. I would have to go to the grandson.

His house is through the woods beyond this inn. Not so far if you're young, but if you're old then, believe me, you count every step and you stumble over every rock and root that crosses your path. At least in the woods it was cool. But when I got to the rebbe's courtyard, people were crushed together on every side—beggars, cripples, and sick people—and the sun was beating down. There were several benches, but every space was filled. I decided to push my way through to the door, and there I found three treasurers sitting. I gave one of them, a man with a big black beard, a ruble and he went in to the rebbe and told him my name. I was lucky. The rebbe remembered me from when I was in constant attendance on his grandfather and he wanted me to come to him at once.

I hardly recognized him when I saw him. The last time he was about eight, and now he was seventeen—still with a high voice, but on his chin he had a few hairs. He came over, threw his arms around me, and was overjoyed. When he asked me what my problem was, I kept hesitating, but finally I decided, what's the use? His grandfather was dead. So I showed him the letter and confided everything. The answer he gave amazed me. I was supposed to go to the general. When I left, the walk didn't trouble me this time; I had other things to think about. I reflected. What else was there to do besides what the rebbe said? The sooner I got it over with the better, so when I passed the manor I turned up the path.

There I found a lot of noise and a lot of dust. Workers were ripping down an old lodge where a caretaker had lived. They shouted to each other and threw planks about. At the house three men stood on the roof putting up a scaffold, and below in the garden there were peasants with hoes clearing away old plants. I thought,

"See, the general intends to rip out everything that was before his time." I wasn't surprised he was making all these changes. He was retired and I suppose he intended to spend his time playing cards, hunting, and entertaining guests, and if people were coming he needed a lot of improvements.

I saw a servant come out of the house, so I hurried over to him and tapped his arm. "Please," I said, "I would like to see the general." He turned, brushed off his arm where I touched him, and looked at me as if he could not believe his ears—that an old Jew was asking to see the general. I took the letter out and showed him. Then he agreed to let me follow him into the house.

We went into a big hall with a chandelier overhead and then up a marble staircase. It was just like a palace to me, thick rugs, satin drapes in the windows, paintings and ikons on the walls. I started to wonder how I dared to come into such a place, but it was too late to turn back. The servant took me from room to room. How can I describe the riches I saw? I thought if a general lives this way, what is it like for the czar?

We came to a big salon with couches and chairs covered with blue silk. The general sat writing at his desk with a white plume. He was a fat, balding man with a pink face, sagging, bloated cheeks like a bulldog's, and little lips like two sausages. Tiny red veins stood out on the bulb of his nose. As he wrote, his nostrils fluttered in and out with uneven, noisy breaths, so I had some idea what noises could be heard in his bedroom when he was asleep. It was a sound like a bull snorting.

As I waited for the general to take notice of me, I wondered what he was writing. Was it another letter similar to the one I held in my hand? Would another poor soul suffer as I did? The general sprinkled some sand on the sheet, then turned his head slightly, hardly glancing at me. This was his polite greeting: "Who are you?"

I replied in a quavering voice, "Honored landlord, I received this letter in regard to the inn. Why do I deserve this? I lived in this place more than seventy years and it has been in my family for a few generations. . . ."

Before I could finish, he said, "I don't want to hear anything. I am asking you one thing, and answer it. Will you sign the contract? Yes or no?"

"No."

I got frightened because all of a sudden he came rushing across the room with big steps, snatched the letter from me, and crumpled it up. Then he told me, "You can go look for another place to live. You can't stay here any longer. Even if you gave me ten thousand rubles. Now leave this house right away."

I started backing away and as I did, I knocked into something so hard, I almost fell down. Don't ask *what* it was, but *who* it was. My enemy, Heschel Goldfarb. He was all wrapped up in a long black cloak. If it was to conceal his sins, or that he too was a Jew, I do not know. He gave me an ugly grin that said, "I see you don't think much of me, but I have my revenge on you, don't I?"

So, my dear guests, what happened next? I received an eviction notice. I had lived in this place from birth on, and now I must take up the wandering stick and go looking. My daughter, who is a widow, must do the same. I did not know where to go, so the days passed and I still had not packed. Since I stayed on, I received a subpoena to go to trial and so I had to hire a lawyer.

It was not easy. I was a Jew, and he was a Russian general; the case looked hopeless. I went as far as Tarnopol, and when I could not find someone to defend me there, I went to Lemberg and still could not hire anyone. Finally, after a month, a lawyer consented to help me, and in good time because I had to appear in court the next day.

What was it like at court? In one room the judge made his pronouncements, and in another they squeezed everybody together, not only the defendants who would be tried, but lawyers and witnesses too. As we waited, one person whispered to another and all kinds of last-minute negotiations took place. Soon the janitor came over and received a tip for himself and then took some money and carried it to someone else. In this way several cases were settled before the trial, including that of a young Jewish couple who sat across from me, who were accused of selling brandy. Only two of the witnesses to testify against them were present to benefit from what the janitor brought over. Their third accuser had died a week before the trial.

I sat quietly and tried to be patient. Next to me was an old Jewish woman, about eighty-five years of age. She kept wringing her hands and trembling. Her arms were thin like twigs and she was blind in one eye. I was curious to know what crime she committed, so I said, "What's your trouble?" This was her answer: She covered her face and started to cry. I really felt sorry for her. "Here's a half ruble" I said to the janitor. "Bring this woman a glass of water." She received it gratefully. Then I told her, "Don't worry so much, because it doesn't help."

"I have reason to worry."

"Maybe it's not so bad as you think."

"It's bad . . . very bad."

Gradually I found out what had happened. She had a fancy goods store, and a gymnasium student came in and bought some gloves. He gave her some money and she gave him the exact change, but he insisted she had to give him a ruble more. Instead of giving the money, she told him what she thought of him. It happens he was of noble descent and could not tolerate insults, and so he went to get the police to arrest her. The result was that now she awaited her fate. I tried to comfort her and told her no one would punish her for a little indelicate language, and no one would send such an old woman to jail. I was certain what I said was true, because the judge had only to take a look at her to see that she would not survive in jail.

More than two hours passed before the court clerk came out and informed me I should be prepared because my case was coming up soon. First the Jewish couple who had sold brandy were going before the judge, then the old woman sitting next to me, and then I would follow. The clerk signaled that the couple should follow him and, along with the defense lawyer and the peasant witnesses, they went into the court. In a little while the whole waiting room became silent because the judge was screaming so loud, and what we heard was "You filthy Jews . . . you vermin." He was infuriated because the first witness had crossed himself and said, "I swear by God's mother, the Virgin Mary, that the other son of a bitch who died a week ago made us bring false charges. This couple is innocent." The second peasant said exactly the same thing. Even when the judge asked, "Who bribed you?" the peasants kept to their story, and for this reason he had to let the couple go. When the old Jewish woman went in to be tried, he sentenced her to six months. I was next and it did not take him long to reach a decision. I lost the case and was given a date when I was supposed to move.

I went back to my rebbe. His eyes were glowing because he had been fasting for a week and praying constantly. When I told him I lost the case, he was not troubled. He said, "Appeal to a higher court." To me this advice seemed a little impractical, and I was debating with myself whether to follow it. You know who helped me decide? Heschel Goldfarb. He came to me and said, "It's a sin to waste money on another lawyer. Give me two hundred rubles and I'll take care of things. Don't appeal the case." I thought, does an enemy give good counsel? I better do the opposite.

After I lost at the higher court I visited the rebbe again. As usual he received my news calmly. He said, "Now you must go and plead with the general." I answered, "Rebbe, he doesn't want to see my face again. What if he does me injury?" With a serene expression he went over to a window and opened it. "What do you see?" I told him I saw trees and a garden and the rebbe's courtyard. He said, "Just as you see these things, have faith that God looks after you."

His words did not inspire me. I sat here at the inn and did nothing, until finally only one day remained before the eviction. I realized I was more terrified of losing my home than of the general, so I dragged myself to the manor. Again the same servant led me upstairs. The general did not conceal the disgust the sight of me caused him. I bowed low before him, touched my head to the floor, and said, "My lord . . . my landlord . . . have pity on my old age." My words filled him with a terrible rage. His face became really red and the veins on his neck were bulging. "Accursed Jew, even if an unnatural death should overtake me, I still won't have you on my estate."

When I heard these words I began to hurry out of the room, but on the way, I saw him rush over to the fireplace. He picked up a poker, lifted it over his head, and began to come after me. I went out in the hall and to the stairs. I barely saw where I was going; it's a miracle I didn't fall down. Every moment I thought my head was going to be smashed in, but I got safely out of the manor. When I came home, my daughter was frightened because I was trembling so much. She put me in my bed and I stayed there for several hours.

Before the day was over I forced myself to get up and went to a neighbor's to beg him to take my daughter in for a few weeks. In this way I prepared for what was to come. The next morning I did not wait for the constable to arrive, but went out on the road with my sack. I would have hurried by the manor, but something caught my attention. I no longer heard the sound of the carpenters' hammers. When I looked toward the house I noticed all the workers were gone. Then I saw the door open and saw some men carrying what looked like some boards out. They loaded their burden into a coach. Several other people came out of the house, all dressed in black. I felt frightened. I had to know what had happened and went closer. No one noticed me when I went around to the back of the house. There I found a boy feeding the dogs inside the fence of the kennels. I called to him, "What's going on?" He came toward me with a sly look. "The general is dead." I didn't have to ask how, because the moment I heard the news, I knew.

I was no longer afraid of anything in this world. I returned home and no one troubled me. After a week passed, the general's widow summoned me to her. She was dressed in the deepest mourning, a black gown and a long, black veil covering her yellow hair. A heavy cross hung from a silver chain around her neck. I offered her my sympathy for her loss, and she thanked me in a courteous voice. Then she informed me that her brothers had discovered that Heschel Goldfarb was a thief. They advised her to have him arrested, but she decided it was better to release him to meet his own fate. All the while I saw she was carefully studying my face. She said to me, "I understand you are an honest person and I want to know if you would like to have the position of manager of my estate that the other Jew had?" I accepted.

So, my guests, now you understand why we have a little celebration in honor of my rebbe this evening.

It was quite late now, and all the guests, including myself, went to our rooms and went to sleep.

I woke early, but not early enough. Mendel and Itze had driven off without me. The mistress came over when I was tying on my *tefillin,* and when I finished my prayers she told me not to worry, one of the guests was going to Acrotchme and would give me a lift. I spent the day being jostled in a wagon, and when it became dark I was let off at another inn.

Here I received a different reception from the day before. A slovenly Jewish woman met me at the door and chased me away because she didn't like my looks. When no one was looking I crept into the stable and slept with the animals. In the morning I brushed myself off and started out on the road.

I was fortunate, for a peasant came by and offered me a lift. With him I went about five versts, and afterward I did not have to walk long before someone else gave me a ride. It only lasted a short while and then I was on foot again. Well, it was not so bad. I liked this new landscape. Gone were the gloomy forests and the dark, weathered wooden houses. Here everything was sunny and open. The fields were soft, green, and rolling, dotted with occasional whitewashed houses of stucco with thatched roofs. The peasants were richer here for the soil was better and the growing season longer. They seemed friendlier to strangers and waved to me. One let me stop and rest at his house. How bright the interior was—its white walls decorated with paintings of flowers and grapes, its windows hung with towels with red hems, a colorful rug on one wall and a pair of red trousers thrown across a bar. A pleasant fragrance came from the bouquets of flowers tied to the beams and the soft grasses that covered the floor.

I resumed my journey. I passed a river with some men fishing, saw a man walking with a sleek brown and white cow. Two small boys drove by me in a tiny child's cart, one of them with a small whip which he snapped above his head. I lay down to rest just near an orchard of trees loaded with apples. I slept for about an hour, and when I woke I saw a beggar, an old man, leaning over me. "Where are you going?" he asked. I told him and found I had someone with whom to walk.

He was not the most cheerful companion. As we went through a beautiful setting, he harangued me on how pitiful the conditions of Jews were.

"The world has never seen such suffering as there is among the Jews. One has lost everything in a pogrom; another has all his possessions confiscated by the government, and another has been evicted from the home where he lived for years. Where can justice be found? How will we endure? In nearly every Jewish village half the people are paupers. . . ."

His sad mood was beginning to infect me, and I was glad when he went off and we parted ways. After this I got a lift as far as the outskirts of Razdiolny, the town to which Mendel was going to take me. My plan was that I would sleep on a bench at the terminal there and take a train to Kishinev the next morning.

I saw a farmhouse and went up to ask directions to get to the town. A Jewish woman with a felt kerchief on her head came to the door. We started talking and she wanted to know where I was going. When I told her, she said, "You're not sleeping on a bench tonight. You're sleeping here. Tomorrow my husband will take you to buy your train ticket."

The family consisted of the parents and three children, and I spent a pleasant evening with them. They showed me every kindness, and even gave me a shirt that belonged to the eldest boy. The next day the farmer hitched his wagon and took me to the terminal. Before I parted from him he said, "Write me how they treat a strange boy in yeshiva. I want to know because I pay a lot of contributions to them. Not just me, but everyone around here."

Three bells rang and I boarded the train, the first one I had ever ridden on. I did not manage to get a seat by the window, but I craned my neck so I could see everything. The countryside flew by before my eyes. It amazed me that I was going so fast. After a couple of hours the train went over a bridge, and I saw a wide river, larger than any I had ever seen. I asked the woman beside me what it was, and just as I thought, she answered, "The Dneister."

I knew I was already halfway to my destination. A sense of triumph came over me that I had gotten so far by myself. I had learned that a traveler is in God's eye more than others. People liked to help someone who was unfamiliar, but sometimes mistreated those to whom they had been hardened by habit. Later, when I traveled to America, I was less afraid than others because I remembered how as a child I had been preserved in this long journey.

4

From the cold north
to the sunny south

KISHINEV, 1889–1890

CAN YOU BELIEVE that there was once a city where no Jew went
hungry or went about poorly clothed? A pauper need only apply
at the *shul* and there he would find matrons clamoring to take him
home to share the dinners they had cooked. A beggar was treated
as the most honored guest. After he had been filled with delicious
food and wine, if there was an extra bed he was invited to stay—
and if not, he could return to the *shul* and sleep on one of the
benches.

It is true such a city existed. And its name was Kishinev.

When I arrived at the terminal I was too frightened to ask directions. I stood bewildered by the ringing bells, the piles of luggage,
the porters, the droshky drivers bidding against each other for passengers, the barking dogs, the people rushing here and there—
White Russians, Tartars, Turks, and Jews. Here was a man with
baggy pants, a shirt with full sleeves, and a white turban with a
red crown; there was a man dressed in the Austrian style in a suit
and homburg hat and smoking a cigar.

A Jew took pity and asked me what was the matter. I asked him
if the yeshiva was far. I intended to spend the night sleeping on a

bench there and to present myself the next morning, rested, and with my letter, to the school superintendent.

"Yes, very far," he said.

He looked me over and saw the tears about to spill from my eyes. He took me to a droshky. When I protested that I could not pay, he gave the driver directions and also the fare.

I had barely thanked him when already I was on my way and catching glimpses of a city that was completely different from Proskurov with its narrower winding streets and gray buildings. I saw parks with fountains and statues, and lovely open squares. Most of the buildings were of a sparkling white limestone, and the broad streets were lined with trees, two, three, or even four deep. The Turks had occupied Kishinev until recently, and here and there I saw houses that were pink, green, or bright blue and decorated in front with white plaster ornaments, and the windows were not square but arched in the Turkish style.

At last we arrived at the courtyard of the *shul* and the driver let me off. I went through a beautiful iron filigree gate which had a design that looked like an upside-down menorah. The caretaker was lighting a lamp with a long pipe with a flame at the end. The *shul*, to my astonishment, was all pink, with white plaster rosettes and curlicues all around the arches of the windows.

Inside was a blaze of colors: white curtains with big red roses embroidered on them, pillars painted a swirl of pink and green to look like marble, red velvet carpets, large paintings on the ceiling of a crab, a well, a fish, a bow and arrow, a tiger, and a hawk. A large gold menorah stood in front on a velvet-covered table. On either side of the Holy Ark was marvelously delicate gold filigree formed like a tree, and in its branches were animals and fruits. It was gorgeous. I had never seen or even dreamed of anything like it. It was a long time before I settled in my corner to sleep.

I was exhausted from my trip, and soon my eyes were closed and my dreams, not surprisingly, were of the Garden of Eden, and in it were golden birds, and lions with sparkling ruby eyes. I even saw the beggar who complained so bitterly of Jewish poverty, but he smiled, and was dressed in a red velvet robe, the same brilliant hue as the *shul* carpet. Everything was red or gold in my dream, and it

was so pleasant an atmosphere that it was painful when the sounds
of talking assaulted my ears. I tried to hold on to my sleep, but
could not.

I opened my eyes, and saw a strange sight. Amid the luxury of
the *shul* were some beggars, three men and a woman. Each one
was draped comfortably over a different pew. The woman glanced
at me awhile, then dismissed me from her thoughts, as the others
already had.

One of the beggars was a small, wiry man who went from complaining loudly to weeping piteously. He held his head in his
hands, cried, and sniveled. I wanted to ask what was wrong and
console him, but hesitated because I was only a child.

The man kept wailing, "They won't give them back," and the
others like a chorus answered, "They will. They will."

They talked in this way far into the night, yet I could never
make out what the problem was. Finally the woman stretched out
on one bench and two of the men foot-to-toe on another, and went
to sleep. Only the one who had cried stayed awake, pacing the
aisles and cracking his knuckles. I could not sleep; I looked at the
shul clock and saw it was two, and then three, and then four in the
morning.

Finally I went up to the beggar and said, "Are you sick? Does
your stomach hurt with cramps?" He only moaned. "Do you want
me to warm a brick in the oven to place on your stomach?" He
looked away and cracked his knuckles. So he did not want to pay
attention to a boy. I went quietly back to my bench, lay down, and
slept.

At five o'clock a young man was shaking me awake and telling
me it was time for the morning services; I would have to vacate
my bench. I awoke in confusion. At first I could not even remember where I was—back in Proskurov or in Shumsk. But in a few
moments I recognized the *shul*. All around me were men in white
talaysim and yarmulkes who had begun their prayers. I saw the
beggar praying in back and I was hopeful that his sickness had
passed from him. If not, surely one of the congregation would take
him to a doctor.

I dismissed him from my mind and absorbed myself in the familiar prayers, hoping to forget for a while that I was hungry, that I felt lonely and strange, and that in a little while I would have to go before the superintendent of the school. What if he thought I was not good enough for yeshiva? Without funds how would I get home again? Could my parents bear the sorrow of my failure? I prayed ardently that God would fortify me.

The services ended. I was about to go out when my attention was caught by the beggar again. A group of young men had surrounded him and one held up a pair of *tefillin* and said, "Here they are. Hold on to them." The beggar seized them from his hand and then looked about wildly. Suddenly he scampered away and dove down into the space beneath the tile stove. First there was the sound of something tearing as if he were ripping apart the *tefillin* and then a wailing arose which echoed through the cavity of the stove, "*Oy vey*, they're not the same."

One of the young men crawled beneath the stove and dragged the beggar out, dusty, soiled, and struggling. One in the crowd said to him, "The *tefillin* are yours. Yesterday someone noticed that your *tefillin* were sewn with white instead of black thread. We began to wonder—if the seams were sewn with the wrong thread, perhaps the scripture inside was faulty too. We understood a poor Jew could never afford to have his *tefillin* sent to a scribe to be checked over, and so we took them away from you and did it ourselves. When the scribe opened them up, instead of the scriptures he found eight hundred stinking rubles. We had the proper scripture inserted and now they are kosher."*

The beggar tried to run away, but he was informed he must go to a *rav*, and if he did not submit to the authority of a Jewish judge then the Russian police would be called in to consider the case. The beggar was soon persuaded to comply.

And it was not just the beggar who was to be dragged before the *rav*, but the other three beggars and myself included. It was thought since we had spent the night together that we were all part of the same gang. I was ashamed and could not hold my head up as we were taken through the streets. My parents had sent me

* Kosher: lawful; proper (informal usage).

here with such fervent hopes that I would become a great scholar. Now on my second day in Kishinev I was being treated as a thief. What would become of me? I knew not a single soul to help me.

Word had spread through the city and everyone was curious. When we arrived at the *rav's*, a large crowd squeezed after us into his study. I was jostled from all sides. Someone pulled me up to the front of the room where I stood with the other beggars.

People fell silent out of respect when the *rav* entered the room. When I saw him, I recalled that the study of the Talmud was said to bring beauty to the features. His skin was smooth, his beard a snowy white, and his eyes were dark and piercing, and with those eyes I thought he could see deep into the heart and see all sin. The *rav* called the first three beggars in turn to speak with him quietly and they were able to clear themselves. Then the one with the *tefillin* went up. He whined and cried and tried to vindicate himself. He said he had a wife and daughter in a far-off village who lived in poverty. When the time came for his daughter to get married he had no dowry, and so he came to Kishinev to try to raise it. He had not stolen the money but collected it kopeck by kopeck and then hidden it. His intention was to use the money for a good purpose, to marry off his daughter.

When he finished, the *rav* said, "The Talmud tells us that if a man has fifty rubles and still takes charity, then that man is not to be considered a decent person. How could you have possessed so much money and still left your wife and child without support?" His judgment was that part of the money should be used to buy a train ticket for the man to return to his village and the rest should be sent to the *rav* of his village to be turned over to the wife.

I could hear many loud complaints in the crowd. "Our charity and good deeds turn people into beggars." "This is what we get for our generosity. People make fools of us."

The *rav* turned pale. He cried out in a stern voice, "Not everyone is a degenerate. One should not lump together the innocent and guilty." It was clear his words made an impression. If the people of Kishinev had contemplated releasing themselves from the obligations of charity, the idea was now obliterated.

Finally I was called forward. I remembered my letter from Reb

Berinen and gave it to the *rav*. He read it over, then sighed as he
looked at my shabby clothes and ripped boots. He said, "Go to the
shul, young man, and wait there. Shortly we will take care of you
and all your troubles."

Indeed, they did so. I was fed, I was dressed in new clothes.
"Days" were assigned to me—that is, for each day of the week a
different family took responsibility for giving me dinner. People,
discovering I was friendless, befriended me. I was told over and
over, "Whenever you want, come to our home. Consider it as your
own." I enrolled at yeshiva and was placed in the highest class
with Abraham Ber, a Karliner Hasid and a God-fearing man. He
was not inclined to anger. Gently he won respect and love from
the hundreds of students who studied with him.

I saw that Kishinev was a city of charity.

The households that gave "days" to the yeshiva boys were generally the wealthiest. I found myself in homes where I dried my
hands on the finest linen, drank from golden goblets, ate delicacies, and tasted wine for the first time. I was an awkward village
boy, but I do not think I shamed myself in these rich houses. One
of my hosts said to me, "You have a natural grace." After I accustomed myself to all this, it was hard to imagine that I had once
lived in a backward little town.

In Proskurov, with my relatives, I had seen only wealth. In Kishinev I saw beauty. Here people used their money in ways my
aunt and uncle could never imagine. This was a cosmopolitan city
affected by styles from all over the world. One of my patrons had a
conservatory, an elaborate wood and glass building with a dome,
in which he grew African orchids. Another hired an orchestra to
play—four viols, a cello, three trombones, two flutes, a bass, clari-
net, and drum. Yet another collected oil paintings, large canvases
that took up whole walls. The subjects of these paintings were for-
eign lands, corsairs with their slave women, the city of Venice—
gondoliers on black water with a big pink sky in the background.

As for the conversation, I think poor Simcha Godels from
Shumsk would have been first delighted, then overwhelmed. All
the latest ideas were picked apart and debated.

"You and your *Haskalah** movement . . . ready to drag us all into corruptions. You want the Jews to become Russians, but Jews should become more Jewish. They will never be accepted here, and Zionism is the only answer," a dignified visitor from Jerusalem addressed a fellow guest at a home where I was receiving my meal.

He spoke in Hebrew but was answered in Russian by a gentleman with ultrarefined manners: "Why antagonize people by practicing customs from the fifteenth century? The Jews can't hide in the Holy Land—they are going to have to come out into the modern world, and the sooner the better. The first step is to assume the same language, clothes, and customs as the countries in which they live."

The debate went on hotly that evening, strictly in Russian and Hebrew. The only agreement was that Yiddish was a contemptible "jargon" that should not be spoken. But finally both opponents got so excited that they forgot themselves, and when it came to shouting insults, Yiddish seemed the best language after all.

America was discussed everywhere also. By now everyone seemed to have a relative who had gone there and had a pressing interest. One evening when I was receiving my meal, I met a yeshiva student named Napthali, a tall, yellow-skinned boy with dark hair and eyes who kept his head down and ate in quick gulps. I did not think he was listening to the conversation, but suddenly, with his head lowered still and his mouth half full, he blurted out, "In America the same problems will exist as here in Europe—and the Holy Land isn't the answer either." He looked up all at once in a defiant, challenging way. "A new beginning has to be made—for Jews and goyim alike. The old has to be wiped out. . . ."

"I don't want anarchism disputed here," the host interrupted quickly. "Is this what they discuss at yeshiva? What companion has been filling your head with such ideas?"

Napthali did not answer.

When I left the house, he came up from behind me.

"May I join you?" he asked.

---

* Enlightenment; the movement for intellectual emancipation and secular education among Jews.

He slouched along beside me but did not say much, just made some comments about what a good meal it had been, and complained bitterly about the butcher where he took his Tuesday meals and how he only got the scraps. He wanted to know if I was being cheated on any of my "days."

After talking with him on several occasions, and always on this same subject, I decided that a person with his preoccupations was not very likely to be a revolutionary.

My days were arduous. No one worked as hard as a yeshiva student. We studied, prayed, and fasted constantly. There were countless nights I did not sleep at all. At times it produced states of ecstasy in me, but at other times I felt irritable and could barely drag myself around. The examinations were unending and merciless. The teacher would state some complex, paradoxical problem and one of the students would have to work it out, knowing all the scholarly commentaries that had come before and adding some insights of his own. It seems the whole city learned the results, from the most respected elders to the poorest beggars, and those boys who were most successful were treated well.

The housewives would come to yeshiva and wait respectfully at the gate as if something momentous were going on inside. Along with them they brought kettles of tea, packets of hot pancakes, kasha, pickles, melons, and fresh rolls. I never knew when the janitor would come up to me unobtrusively, interrupt my studies, and signal me to follow him. He would take me to a private room and there I would find that one of the women had left me a delicious meal and also several kopecks to use for the bathhouse or whatever else I needed. On another day, perhaps because I was discoursing poorly, I would be neglected and had no midday meal. This happened rarely.

I never regretted the time I spent studying, never resented it when my eyes burned and my shoulders ached from being stooped over books. My love for Rabbi Abraham Ber grew. When he entered a room, to me it was as if a celestial being had come from the heavens, and suddenly the world was clear, simple, full of light. It was a privilege to be near this saintly man and give him my adulation. How many teachers can arouse this uplifting feeling?

From all his years of instructing students, he had distilled one teaching method, and it was this: telling parables. We gathered around him eagerly in the small classroom. As he talked he snapped his eyes open and shut in a special way to communicate his pleasure. He was not a large man, but pale, hollow-chested, delicate-looking. His beard was scanty and his clothes hung on him.

One time I had been delayed and came in late when he was at the end of one of these parables. I slipped into my seat and felt depressed that I was missing something that would never be written down and that I could never experience again. Even if one of the other students retold it to me, it would not be the same if it came from lips less pure than my teacher's—the tone of his voice, the look in his eye, all helped to convey his meaning.

When the class ended, Abraham Ber came over to me and asked if I wanted him to repeat the tale. Another man would have been offended that I missed his lesson, but this one looked into my thoughts and feelings to see how he could please me.

I am sure he had much else to do, but he would not convey to me that he was hurried. He sat beside me, and began:

"Chaim Berlin, the great nineteenth-century Talmudic scholar, was traveling about—not, God forbid, to demand personal contributions, or deal in magic, but simply to gather money for the Volsziner yeshiva. During his journeys he came to the city of Balta where there lived a butcher, a poor man. The butcher would eke out a livelihood with money that kind people lent him, and he would go off to a village, buy an animal, and then have it slaughtered in the city. As soon as this was done, he would have to repay the loans, and sometimes something was left over for him. During the time Chaim Berlin was visiting, the butcher had an animal killed. The *shochetim** saw that the animal's lung did not look healthy; yet they did not have the heart to tell the butcher that it

* Plural of *shochet,* or ritual slaughterer.

was not kosher, and so they decided to take it to the *rav* and let the responsibility fall to him to inform the butcher that the meat must be thrown away. They carried the carcass, and the butcher, poor thing, went along, just like a mourner following a corpse.

"The *rav* too could not bring himself to tell the butcher the bad news. So he said to the *shochetim,* 'You know what, go ask this difficult talmudic question of Harav Chaim Berlin.'

"They left and again the poor butcher followed behind. When they came to Chaim Berlin and demanded that he judge whether the animal was kosher, he asked, 'Who is the man standing by the door?' He was informed that it was the butcher. He considered him a few minutes and said, 'When the compiler of the Halakah* wrote the laws, the butcher did not stand opposite him. I, who do see the butcher, rule that it is kosher.' "

I thanked my teacher and told him I was deeply grateful.

He took such delight in telling tales to his students. Now that I consider the matter, I realize that I owe much to his influence that I am capable of writing down my memories.

I liked to take long walks through the city at night, to look into the lighted windows at the life illuminated within. Only at night could I pause unobserved and see what it was like in the elegant restaurants, or how it was in the salons of wealthy Russian homes where people danced or played cards. I liked to stroll along the River Bik past Mazaraki Church, which had once been a mosque, or to wander through the gardens of Pushkin Park.

Once, as I was loitering like this, I came upon the yeshiva student Napthali deep in conversation with another boy. A disturbing feeling filled me when I saw them; I was trying to remember something, but I could not. I was about to pass them by, but Napthali called out, "David, come meet my friend Moishe."

The other boy put out his hand to shake mine in a friendly way. He was eighteen years old and a head taller than I, dressed in a gymnasium student's uniform with silver buttons and a cap. If I

---

* Jewish law, including oral law as transcribed in the Talmud, and subsequent codes amending the traditional laws.

had seen him along the street I would not have guessed that he was Jewish. He was tall, with wavy blond hair and trimmed *peyes*. His eyes were blue, his features regular.

From the first I was struck with what an intelligent person he was. Of course, for a Jew to be admitted to a Russian gymnasium, he had to be brilliant. His mannerisms were nervous. He walked fast. He spoke quickly and made jabbing gestures with his hands for emphasis.

Gradually, Napthali was left out of the conversation. He wasn't able to keep up with the exchange of ideas. Moishe began to address himself exclusively to me. I was flattered by this attention from an older boy. I listened to him discussing historic events and dates I had never heard about and was inspired with curiosity and awe. Here was the gymnasium student, Simcha Godels's ideal. What great future was before him? Would he soon be moving among the Russian aristocracy?

I did not want to part from him, but it became late. I went to sleep on the bench at the *shul* and in the morning resumed my studies. When I recalled this encounter, it was with a sad feeling that I would not meet this fascinating young man again. Why should a gymnasium student like him show any further interest in me?

At the end of the week I was called out of my classes for an interview with a woman. "I believe you know my son Moishe," she said.

"Yes."

"Well, you made such a favorable impression on him that he suggested you take your board at our house several days a week."

I was astonished and joyful. Almost daily I would see Moishe. I felt he would become a closer friend to me than any I had ever had.

Monday, I made my way to Moishe's house, a two-story, white stucco building. The servant, an old crone, decked out in a colorful skirt and ruffled petticoat, chatted with me in a friendly way and led me into the house. We ate at once. The table was presided over by Chaim and Naomi Goldstein. Besides Moishe, there was a daughter of sixteen years. There was a warm friendly atmosphere.

The parents had married late in life and had not expected to have any children. They were overjoyed with Moishe and Rifka. One or the other of the parents kept asking me in a whisper, wasn't Moishe brilliant? Wasn't Rifka beautiful? Did I ever see such fine children? Since I nodded with sincere enthusiasm, they found me agreeable. In the midst of such tenderness I began to miss my own parents.

Later I went to Moishe's room. I had my yeshiva books and he had his from the gymnasium to study. He looked mine over and began debating with me in Hebrew. I was impressed. In the yeshiva he would have been the best student. Yet I sensed that my teacher Abraham Ber would not have been pleased with him. He would have found him too intellectual. But to me, he was dazzling.

I could not resist picking up some of Moishe's books. There was the one on algebra I had studied with Simcha Godels. My friend was surprised when he saw me leafing through it.

"Can you do those problems?"

"Yes . . . several."

He took the mathematics book and pushed it away. "Here, take these," he said and brought over history and literature books, the subjects that interested him most. The authors I began to read after this were Dostoevski, Turgenev, and Pushkin. It was the first time I read novels, a new and exciting experience, particularly because my friend guided me.

In many ways it was like the Shumsk Bes Medresh, where the one that was proficient taught the other. Just as we did with Torah, we memorized whole passages—those which Moishe had selected as being important. We recited to each other and had long discussions about the meaning of some point the author was making.

I was imbibing worldly knowledge again, and this time from an extraordinary teacher. Somehow it did not seem harmful, and if my conscience was troubled, it was only a little. This was a weakness I had of which I never seemed able to be cured. Usually our discussions went on long into the night; then Naomi herself would come in with bedding and make a place for me to sleep on the couch.

There were times when I found my friend in a depressed mood, and he confided in me that he felt like an outcast at the gymnasium. Students and teachers alike found ways to torment him because he was a Jew. No one spoke to him. He was asked to stand during classes. One teacher had even resorted to changing some of his answers from right to wrong on a written examination.

I never could predict his moods. Sometimes it seemed to me that there was much more troubling him than he confided. He had to be alone, for any presence, even mine, troubled him. He said, "You're too pious to talk to, David. I'd rather be with Napthali, except that he's not as intelligent as you." Sadly, because I valued his company so much, I would leave. I walked through the streets back to the *shul*.

I never minded it when I lacked a soft bed and had to sleep on the *shul* benches, because several of my yeshiva comrades slept there. We had formed a circular chorus. We would practice hymns just before we went to sleep, and the beggars of Kishinev were our audience. To my ears, our high, boyish voices were excellent. The singing put us all in good spirits. So what if the benches were hard? I really liked these boys, but to none of them did I feel the same closeness as to Moishe. I loved him with all my heart and even when we were separated I was thinking about him. My last thought upon retiring was of my friend and that I would have much preferred to spend the evening talking with him.

I wrote to my parents, "I am warm and well fed, and I study merrily." I did not want them to worry, just as I never did. But it was not my mother's way not to worry.

She wrote back, "Russia, dear child, has become a cauldron." Stories of the dangers and unrest in the cities spread even to Shumsk. Mystics sprang up here and there promising a better life. She was fearful I might fall victim to one, Yossel Rabinowitz, who roamed about Russia proselytizing among the young for his new sect. Even more she feared the underground societies. More and more Jewish youths were joining these groups and holding surreptitious meetings, which were frequently raided by the police. When I first came to Kishinev I was unaware this was going on, but after a while it was impossible not to hear some of the frightened whisperings—an aristocrat's son, or even a daughter, had been arrested; the son of a distinguished Jew suddenly disappeared. It was said that the police did not bother to investigate too carefully, and often the innocent were dragged away and executed.

Among the small group of Jewish students at the gymnasium, there were several accused of being Nihilists. Perhaps this was true, as they were exposed to a more secular life than the yeshiva boys. When four were arrested it made me fearful for my friend Moishe. I did not suspect him of being politically active. I was simply afraid that the goyim in his school would revenge themselves on him for the faults of others. However, weeks passed and he was safe.

Such horrors as these I did not let myself dwell on long. I wrote what I thought was a learned-sounding letter to my mother to assure her that there was nothing to fear. My opinion was that the Nihilists were like the son of the tribe of Ephraim who wished to make a premature escape from Egypt and was turned back with great setbacks. To me it seemed that those who joined the Nihilists only endangered their lives and brought pain on their families. Why should I fall into such iniquity? My life in Kishinev could not be better.

One day I wandered into a section of the city that I did not know well. I decided I had better return to yeshiva, and I went up to a peddler who was walking up and down the street selling hats, to ask directions. The moment I opened my mouth he seized me with a powerful grip.

It was Mendel.

He said, "Come on, let's have a drink together, and I won't take no for an answer."

I started to protest. I was resentful because he had left me at the inn. But he talked to me in a friendly way and my anger began to melt. Anyway he would not let me escape and I really had no choice but to go with him.

He pulled me along the street, all the time talking in a loud voice. I felt embarrassed to be with this companion, and when we went past several taverns and the neighborhood became worse, I started feeling anxious. At last we came to our destination, a dilapidated two-story building called the "Grand Hotel" despite its condition. There were a few narrow rooms rented out on top, and down below was an enormous room, part of which was the kitchen.

I was introduced to the landlord and landlady; he was lame and she blind in one eye. Several guests were gathered about a large table. These were poor people, a few peddlers, a porter, a tailor without work, and others. Mendel was given a hearty greeting. He took me around and introduced me to everyone and they made room for us. All these people looked up to me because I attended yeshiva.

I began to enjoy myself, and several hours passed without my even realizing it. Mendel was displaying his considerable talents as a clown. He started to tell a few stories that were not in the best of taste, but when he started hopping around and making faces, I could not hold the laughter back. The landlady was laughing so hard she was choking, and her husband, Beryl, had to slap her on the back, saying, "*Nu*, Feiga, control yourself." Then he took a look at Mendel, and it was Feiga who had to slap his back, saying, '*Nu*, Beryl, you control yourself."

Finally I remembered my class at Yeshiva and that I was late. Everyone tried to persuade me to stay, and they spoke to me so warmly that I really regretted going. The landlord said, "Please come back another time." I said I would try.

I ran back to school. The moment I walked in, the supervisor of the yeshiva, Tzaddik Alyushus, came over to tell me I was late. This man had a pale, weary face. I heard he put beans in his socks, and constantly found new ways to torment his flesh. With a few words and a slight flickering of his eyelid he expressed his irritation with me. It made me feel a little depressed. I went to my studies with less enthusiasm than usual.

A week later I went to visit Mendel again, and this time I enjoyed myself even more. There was something boisterous in my character. I liked to be with simple, hearty people. Maybe it was because in my early childhood I played with the peasant children; or maybe it had something to do with all the restraint I suffered when I lived with Aunt Bobbah and Uncle Nuchem. Anyway, there was a wild part of me that had to be free. I developed a craving to see Mendel and his friends and began to go to his hotel on a regular basis. After, I went back to my studies with the usual ardor.

This was the happiest time in my life; but if the sun rises, it must also set. Shmuel, who slept beside me on the *shul* bench, got sick. At first we thought maybe something he ate disagreed with him and the stomach pains would soon go away. But after two days he was worse. His eyeballs were sunken and his voice weak. His hands and feet started to hurt. I took him to the hospital. At the end of the week when I went to inquire about him, I was informed that he was dead.

Then another boy took sick. He was a member of our choir; he was buried just before the Shabbes.* Then it was another, and another. We were torn between grief and fear for ourselves. The authorities refused to recognize that anything was wrong. One day I would be talking with a boy with fresh cheeks and bright eyes, and that night he would start vomiting and have cramps. Then in five or six days he was dead. I felt as if I was living in a nightmare.

When the son of an important person died, the community finally acknowledged that there was a sickness among us. A committee was appointed to investigate, and they said that it was cholera. They closed the yeshiva down immediately. Since it was thought I might carry the disease, I received letters from all my formerly gracious hosts, "Do not dare to show your face among us." Who would welcome me? Where could I go? It was not practical to travel back to Shumsk, because of the expense and because by the time I got there the yeshiva might reopen.

I decided to go to Mendel. I knew he would not be afraid of the sickness; he was not afraid of anything. I would appeal to him and the owners of the hotel. Poor people would take pity. They would

* The Sabbath.

be more afraid to abandon a child, than they would be of the disease.

It happened just as I thought. I went to the hotel, asked for help, and it was arranged that I would share Mendel's room. We had a tiny space with a wash basin. I got all my meals and a few candles for the night. In exchange for all this, I began tutoring Beryl and Feiga's five-year-old son. Everyone was satisfied.

Beryl said, "I'm saving money, I don't have to hire a teacher."

Only my mother, when she heard, did not like it and wrote, "How can you live with that ruffian Mendel? He would not hesitate to blot you off the face of the earth."

Despite my mother's words I felt my position was satisfactory—until one evening when I was sitting at dinner and Beryl said, "A toast to Mendel, who is having an engagement party here tomorrow night." I started to choke on a morsel of bread. Mendel glared at me, and his look was enough to silence me.

Mendel had a wife already and I knew her. She was living in Shumbar. The first time I had met Mendel in Kishinev he had said to me, "Don't tell anybody I have a wife." I thought nothing of it. First of all, it was not my business, and secondly, no one ever asked me, so I did not have to lie. But now it was different. I had to sit there while Mendel fooled these people. I went to my room to go to sleep, as I did not feel like sharing in the festivities. Mendel followed after and said "Don't tell."

I said, "I certainly won't."

The next night the entire neighborhood showed up for the engagement party, which my landlord was paying for. The poorest beggar was invited. On every side were boisterous people. Mendel was leading the bride around. Poor thing, she was all pockmarked and had crooked teeth, and seemed ashamed to look anyone in the eye. People whispered she had worked hard as a servant and saved a fine dowry to bestow on her groom. The betrothed couple came up to me and the maid said timidly, "Oh, you knew Mendel in Shumbar." Immediately Mendel dragged her away and the crowd closed around them.

People became a little more dignified when the *rav* arrived. To my astonishment it was the same one I had met on the second day I spent in the city. A table was cleared and he began to write the engagement articles with great care, a solemn expression on his features. I almost fainted as I watched him. I wanted to shout to him, "Stop. The law is being desecrated, and with your own hand." The words pounded in my head, but my tongue was still. Sweat was drenching my clothes and I could not take my eyes from him.

I was anxious for the *rav* to leave immediately, but that was not how things turned out. He congratulated the bride and groom. Mendel insisted that he stay and have a sip of brandy, to which the *rav* consented politely. Then Mendel stood there trying to think of some appropriate conversation he could have with this distinguished and learned guest. He kept clearing his throat, but nothing came out. I could see he felt foolish and longed to be released from his agony. His eyes searched the room for a savior, and he noticed me. "Look, Rabbi, here's *my* yeshiva boy," he said in a loud voice and beckoned to me. I was supposed to entertain the *rav* for him.

What could I do? I had to go over. The *rav* remembered me, and he wanted to know how I was doing now that the yeshiva was closed. I told him I was keeping up with my studies independently. He said, "I'm glad to hear this. If you have any questions, do not hestitate to come to my house to consult with me." Mendel was lighting up like a menorah that the *rav* and I were exchanging a few words.

When the *rav* gave this invitation, Mendel had to add, "Don't worry, he will." Finally the *rav* left.

No one noticed when I slipped away to my bedroom. I had to think what to do. It was a grave sin not to expose Mendel, and while there was time. If I did not, then his first wife would become an *agunah.** But still I hesitated. Mendel had helped me and been truly good to me. But even more than that, I was afraid of him.

I was surprised Mendel did not notice how depressed I was. I

---

* *Agunah:* According to Jewish law she would remain married to him and could not take another husband.

suppose he was too busy rushing off to visit his sweetheart. The only precaution he took was to pull me aside in the hallway occasionally, put his finger over his lips, and say, "Remember, *shah!*"*

Several days after the engagement party, I was going down the stairs with a Gemara under my arm and was almost out the door when Mendel grabbed me. This time he was suspicious.

"Where are you going?"

"I have a question for the *rav* who wrote your marriage contract. See this book."

He glanced and saw it was large and heavy, and a look of pleasure came into his eyes.

"Go and send him the best of everything from Mendel, the one who saved you. Tell him I expect him at my wedding."

I ran through the streets like a wild man. When I arrived at the *rav*'s, he could not see me for a while and I had to wait. I paced back and forth, jerked on my *peyes,* and chewed my fingers until they were raw. The *rav* came out and saw the Gemara. "Ah, my child, you have been industrious in your studies."

I said, "No, it's something else."

He looked astounded. Upon entering his study I began to recite the *"Viddui"*† because I felt I was putting my life in jeopardy. When I finished, I told him. All light faded out of his eyes, and his body seemed to fold over. He turned from me to the wall and prayed fervently and long. Then he said softly, "Return at eight and repeat this story to some others whom I will choose to hear what you say."

That night I asked Feiga where Mendel was.

"With his bride."

I went to the *rav's* again. The successful businessmen of Kishinev lounged about, drinking, eating small cakes, and chatting with each other. Only the *rav* was grave. He had me stand in the center of the room and tell my story. I saw my audience took my words lightly; to them I was just a boy who wanted attention. "How do we know you're not just dreaming?" one man said. This

---

* *Shah:* Be quiet!
† *Viddui:* Prayer for forgiveness when one's life is put in jeopardy, or when one is close to death.

drew laughter from about the room. As young as I was, and as important and respectable as were these older men, I felt enraged. I was risking my safety and they were making jokes.

I said, "Forget what I told you. Yes, it's a dream. But if you have a little curiosity, risk spending a ruble and send a telegram to Mendel's hometown."

A telegram was sent to the *rav* living closest to Shumbar. The answer affirmed what I said.

This took two days and I was still living at the hotel. I was terrified that the secret would get out. Frequently I regretted what I had done and tried to form some plan for fleeing Kishinev. But before I could run away, something important happened.

On the third day after my interview with the *rav* there was a raid at the hotel. The police came and everyone was rousted out of bed at two o'clock in the morning. There were about eight guests at this time. We all were lined up in the hall with the hotel owner and had to submit to questioning and have our passports examined. I was one of the first, and they approved mine quickly and then the next, and next, but when the inspector came to Mendel he said, "Your passport has expired."

Mendel answered, "I applied for a new one a few weeks ago and it has not come yet."

The inspector shouted, "What's taking so long? You'd better come with me."

Mendel started to object, but it was futile. The day before, a small committee selected by the *rav* had gone to the authorities and with proper financial inducement had persuaded them that Mendel might benefit from a stay in jail. It seems that sort of thing was always easy to arrange. A certain party could be arrested on the pretext that he did not have the proper red passport ticket. And if he had a red one, well, then he was taken to jail because it should have been blue. Once he was detained, getting all of the records would take a long time. When they had everything, it could even take longer. An official had to digest all the information, and after this was done he passed it on to the next bureaucrat, and meanwhile an innocent man could grow old in jail because there were more bureaucrats in Russia than there were years in a man's life.

When finally they were dragging Mendel away it must have flashed through his mind what had happened, because he glared at me and started muttering. The inspector became curious and asked a guest, "What did he say?" The guest translated it into Russian as best he could. The inspector came up to me and said, "You better watch out. That man is going to cut your guts out at the first opportunity."

By the next morning, the whole story about what had happened had leaked out. I would not say a word to anyone and would have liked to forget it completely. I went for a walk and my ill luck was that I passed by the house where Mendel's fiancée lived. At that moment she was returning from the market and a few idlers had gathered to inform her of the news. Just as she came down the street carrying a package someone yelled out, "Hey, your Mendel is already married!" The girl turned pale and dropped her bag, and potatoes spilled over the cobblestones. "Is it true?"

The crowd was in an ugly mood. A chorus of angry voices rose at the same time, each screaming something else:

"There are too many agunahs already."

"Husbands slip over the border and emigrate to America, and hundreds of wives are left. Who do you think should support them?"

"And what about the children?"

"You think you could sin and not be discovered?"

The girl looked around with a dazed expression. "I didn't know he was married" she said.

I ran up to her, took her hand and pulled her to her door. "Go lock yourself up," I said and gave her a push inside. Then I ran away.

The news I heard later about her astonished me. A whole day she stayed in her house without coming out. When she did, she had dressed herself in her best dress, walked erectly, and had such a desperate, determined look on her face that no one dared interfere with her. First she went to the homes of a few important Jews and made scenes demanding that her lover be released, and from there she ran to the jail. The police considered it a fine joke to abuse her, but finally they realized they would not get rid of her unless they let her in to see Mendel.

What happened between them I cannot know, except it seems they were reconciled and Mendel sent this audacious message out with her: "Jews of Kishinev, if you want me to give my first wife a divorce you will have to pay all the costs, and in addition you will have to get me out of jail at once."

One evening I had just finished dinner and was going through the hallway when I saw a dark shape in the shadows, someone waiting for me there. The first thought that came to mind was that somehow Mendel had been released or escaped. I was so terrified, I simply stood there with my eyes shut, holding my breath and expecting death.

A voice whispered, "You must come with me to the *rav*'s at once." To my relief it was not Mendel but the *rav*'s servant. I followed him without a word, my heart still thudding. He walked rapidly, taking little-used streets. When we came to the *rav*'s house, I ascended the stairs and went inside unaccompanied. I knew the way to the study well by now. When I knocked on the door, the *rav* called, "Come in and close the door behind you."

In one corner stood the *rav* and beside him a young Jew with a broad back and a red face, dressed in the coarse, loose-fitting peasant's costume of Novo Bessarabia. He had a strong odor; it seems he had spent the day at the Kishinev market selling hides.

The *rav* pointed to me. "This is the boy."

His companion, whose name was Hyman Horwitzer, said, "I hope my wife won't drive me out of the house for this surprise."

The *rav* wanted Mendel released—not because Mendel demanded it, but because it was wrong to hold a man in jail on false charges. He told me I had to leave the city with Hyman Horwitzer at once, and later when it was safe for me, he would write and I could return.

Everything was done to ensure that no one would recognize me when I left. I was given some new clothes, and when I changed into them my appearance was somewhat different. I was smuggled out of the city at midnight. The only ones who were informed were my parents. They received a letter from the *rav* reassuring them about my well-being and praising me for having saved a woman from becoming an *agunah.*

I was taken to Cotu Mori on the Romanian border. It was a small village of shepherds and fishermen located beside the River Prut, near a port which was also a border checkpoint, and near an army garrison. The Valachia dialect was spoken in this region, and I found I had no difficulty mastering it. I lived in a one-room peasant cottage. There was a cellar outside, a deep hole in the ground for cool storage, covered by a thatch roof, a few other storage sheds, and a wattle fence with a low step in it so the cattle could step over. The house was stucco and painted orange; those nearby were blue and yellow.

It wasn't luxurious, but it did not matter since most of the time I was outside. I loved to walk along the river, to watch the fishermen casting their nets. "Come on and help out," they called, and so I waded into the water.

The warmer weather came all at once and this pleasure of strolling by the river was ruined for me because on the other shore women came to bathe and exposed their arms and legs. Hyman Horwitzer would tease me, "Did you see anything interesting at the river?" "No," I retorted, "I never go there any more."

Each morning I woke up to the sound of sheep bleating. The flocks were owned communally by everyone in the village. I went out barefoot with the shepherds and walked with a tall crook. My companions were not talkative, so I found it pleasant to daydream—and the one I thought about most often was Moishe. It was just as if he were at my side and I had long conversations with him. He and his family had left the city because of the sickness, and I wondered if they were back in Kishinev yet.

At night, I often stayed with the shepherds to eat my meal, and slept beneath the stars. One shepherd put an iron pot on the fire and boiled milk. Then it was made into a cheese, *kashvel,* that was shared. They lit their pipes and wrapped themselves up in long black cloaks. They taught me their shepherd's songs. Sometimes I went back to Hyman's, and his wife made *mamliga,* a mixture of barley and flour simmered in boiling water. When it cooled she cut it with a thread. I never ate so much lamb or fresh fish in my life, and I never felt healthier. I started to fill out a little. I got taller and my voice became deeper.

During this time Hyman Horwitzer became the partner of a Jew who had the commission for ordering supplies for the garrison. I started going to the port daily. Along the shore sailors and porters unloaded cargo and straining oxen pulled barges to the dock. Since it was the border, there were also army sentries patrolling back and forth. What a contrast there was between the sweating mob of workers and the soldiers dressed in immaculate uniforms. The soldiers wore white tunics, dark trousers, and round peakless hats. Their high boots gleamed like mirrors. They sat erectly on sleek horses and paraded slowly back and forth. I would gaze at them for hours with admiration and envy.

One afternoon a soldier came up to me and said, "I hear you speak the local dialect. I want you to carry a message to the garrison." I was stunned when he led out a piebald horse. He did not ask whether I could ride. I mounted as I had seen the soldiers do; how dizzy it felt to be up so high. I wondered how to make the horse move, but the soldier slapped its rump. It took off. She was not the gentlest animal and realized she was carrying an inexperienced rider. For once her will would be supreme. I was treated to a swift, wild gallop in which I slid all over the horse's back but somehow stayed on.

That I got to the garrison, and that I even remained alive and had not been thrown and trampled, seemed miraculous to me. Perhaps it was because I was at an age when I still had a boy's agility. Yet if I had been a year or two younger, I would not have been strong enough to direct the horse to the garrison. I found in myself a certain physical daring and courage that I had not had before when I was a yeshiva student.

The officer who sent me to the garrison was pleased when I returned quickly. He talked to Hyman and after this the job of messenger was mine. I spent all my time riding. Slowly I learned to ride well, and also how to care for horses.

⁓5

I become a somebody

MY STAY IN Cotu Mori came to an end in this manner: My parents wrote saying they wished me to return to Shumsk and marry Perl. I delayed my departure a few days and in this time received a second letter. It was from the *rav* in Kishinev, who did not know about my parents' wishes. The *rav* told me it was safe for me to come back to Kishinev and he wanted me to live with him until yeshiva opened. The community had decided the most efficient way to get rid of Mendel was to arrange for his release and pay for his divorce. Once Mendel came out of jail, he saw how much everyone despised him and finally he was ashamed to show his face, and he and his bride disappeared.

I decided that instead of going directly to Shumsk, I would travel to Kishinev and beg the *rav* to intercede with my parents for me that they should not make me marry Perl. I rode part of the way and walked the rest, and the trip took nearly two days. It happens I arrived on the day of my birthday. I had experienced a lot in the two years since my bar mitzvah. That had been a turning point in my life, and although I did not realize it, now at fifteen, I was at another.

When we were inside the city we happened to pass my friend Moishe's house, and I called to the coachman to let me down. By

the time he stopped we were a few streets away. I took my knapsack and ran back. I was breathless when the servant let me in.
Even so, I was so excited at the thought of seeing my friend that I
talked to her merrily.

I started chiding the old woman because she was dressed
plainly, all in black, instead of decking herself out in her mistress'
hand-me-down clothes and baubles as she usually did. "Where are
your beads today? Not even a single strand ... and you let your
apron get dirty. Did you know it was my birthday? It's not nice of
you not to wear a flower in your hair in my honor."

It seemed she had taken on a disagreeable character in the time I
was gone. To all my remarks, she said nothing, just led me to a
rather dark room where the shutters were closed, and there I
waited.

Unable to sit still, I paced around, even found myself laughing
aloud. Then I heard footsteps and my heart seemed to rise high in
my chest as I watched the door open. Instead of my friend I saw
his parents. With joy I greeted them. I rushed over and squeezed
Chaim's hands and kissed Naomi's cheeks, and although they did
not respond in kind, I did not take it amiss. I just said happily,
"Where is Moishe?" Silence. The mother went to sit on the couch
and Chaim looked at me with a bewildered expression. "What's
wrong? Were you sick?" I blurted out. A feeling of dread started
to creep over me. "Where's Moishe?"

After what seemed a long time, I heard, "Gone."

Naomi covered her face with her hands. Tears were streaming
from Chaim's eyes. I pleaded with them to tell me what had happened. Slowly the story came out. The police had found political
pamphlets in both Moishe's and his sister Rifka's rooms and they
had been arrested. The parents did not know where they had been
taken; most likely they had been executed. In my excitement I had
not noticed my friend's parents were dressed in black. Now I saw
their somber clothes. Now I saw their pain. I tried to comfort
them, but in the end I saw it was futile. What consolation could be
given? For these people, their life, as well as their children's, was
over. I left them in the darkened room, to sit, to stare, to mourn.

I went out on the street. A weight pressed down on me and I

moved faster and faster as if I could escape it. Wild thoughts rushed through my head. I became furious with Moishe that he had not confided in me he was in an underground organization. Then I thought again of what had happened to him and Rifka, and I was overwhelmed with horror.

I walked past peddlers, stores, taverns, hotels, churches, a *shul*, and on and on. Suddenly I did not want to return to yeshiva, just as I did not want to return home to marry Perl. My whole fate seemed stifling. I would live a life of poverty, and in the end there would be death, just as there had been for Moishe. I wanted an escape and yet it seemed impossible to take one. I had to obey my parents.

Twilight came and the streets emptied. Everything was unfamiliar. I saw a Jew with a large sack and I asked him, "Where am I?"

He answered abruptly, "You are where you don't belong."

After a while I felt little else but exhaustion. I came to a hotel, an old brick building and went inside.

I climbed a flight of stairs and came into a large, well-lit room. The hotel owner, a Jew, was behind a counter drying some dishes with a cloth. I went up to him and said, "I need a room for the night," and then showed him my passport. He looked it over and when he saw my name he became excited.

"I want you to know the room is free, and ask for anything you want."

"What does this mean?"

"You're the one who saved the woman from becoming an *agunah*. Everyone has heard about you, and you are considered a hero."

I had little time to reflect upon this. That moment the downstairs door was pushed open and we heard a loud crash and some furious curses. The hotelkeeper ran down to find out what was going on.

Shortly he appeared with a man in a sheepskin coat, both straining beneath the weight of a huge keg of wine. Four such kegs they brought up. The man bringing up the wine with the hotelkeeper was stout, and this work was hard for him. He kept complaining in a loud voice, "This isn't my work. But what can I do? The damn worker quit today. When my man can't deliver, I must do it. My customers can rely on me. . . ."

When they were finished I was still by the counter waiting for a room. They came up together talking animatedly. The wine dealer said to me, "Hey, are you the one that saved the woman from becoming an *agunah?*"

I answered, "What if I am?"

The man introduced himself as Yankel and said, "Well, I have a job for you."

"What if I don't want it?"

"Just listen to my terms and you can't refuse."

I let him lead me over to a table and sank into a seat. He sat in a chair opposite me and leaned forward eagerly. "I can't read or write, so I can't keep accounts—and believe me, it's no small business. Day and night I'm worried sick that one of my workers is going to steal from me and I won't know. Tonight I came to deliver some kegs and I heard this story about you and the woman you saved. I thought to myself that here was someone who was not only clever but pious as well. I decided in an instant that you and no one else would keep my books."

He waited for an answer, but I just stared at him.

"Well, come and work for me. If you don't like it, after a week I'll bring you back myself." I wanted to go with him, but I knew that I shouldn't, and so I could not form an answer. He had an appointment somewhere else, so he became impatient and said he was going down to his wagon, but I could walk along with him. As we went down the stairs he said, "Believe me, an opportunity like this doesn't come every day."

Only a few hours before I had been glad to see the city, but now the only thing I noticed was the reeking garbage strewn on the street. The whole atmosphere was poisoned for me. Then as we came up to Yankel's wagon I smelled an odor that reminded me of Cotu Mori. I saw a beautiful horse, an Arabian, which to me is the cream of breeds.

She was a powerful animal, of a pure charcoal color, with not a speck of white. I went over to stroke her and my hands were trembling. My fingers moved lightly up and down her back; beneath the thin, flexible skin I could feel the taut, powerful muscles. There was no dust, not a bare spot; the hide was really sleek. The thought passed through my mind that if I got on the horse's back and galloped away, somehow the sick and sad feelings I had would go away too.

"Well will you come? Make up your mind."

"Would I be able to ride the horse?"

"Where did a yeshiva boy learn to ride?" I murmured that I had learned near a garrison.

"Sure, you can ride, if you know how. You'll ride first thing in the morning."

"I'm coming with you." The words tore out of me. I ran inside to get my knapsack. I had to go quickly before the old doubts and hesitations caught up with me.

We went to a tavern. As it turned out, it was only on the outskirts of the city, and I could have gone back at any time by myself. At the tavern I began my employment, was given a white apron to tie over my gaberdine and started taking orders, serving, washing glasses, and collecting money. Most of the customers were workers from a slaughterhouse across the road.

After I had been working a few hours I went to Yankel and asked him permission to go in back to pray. He was overjoyed and said, "Pray as much as you want." My zealousness reassured him that I obeyed the commandments, particularly "Thou shalt not steal." I went to a small room with a bed where I would sleep that night and where I had left my belongings. I took out my *tallis*, shut from my mind the sounds from next door, which were considerable, and said my prayers.

Refreshed in this way I returned to work. Bleary-eyed men screamed for more drinks and toasted each other noisily. The place was packed with people. A fight broke out and knives were drawn, but a few of the more sober ones in the crowd stopped it. It was a rough bunch who came here. I remembered rumors I had heard in the city that whenever anyone needed someone beaten or killed he called upon the tanners from the slaughterhouse.

I slept only a few hours that night. At dawn I went to the stable and opened the door quietly. In the darkness of the barn I saw the Arabian with ears pricked and staring at me. By the way she turned her head and followed my every motion I could see this was an alert, intelligent horse. I had learned to be careful around animals until I saw whether their dispositions were good. As I brought hay and a bucket of water I was more wary than the night before, but the Arabian seemed gentle.

She cooperated when I led her outside and mounted her. Her back was broad and strong and I could grip her tightly with my thighs. Out in the countryside in a large field, I began to ride faster, and kept making new demands on her. Gradually I saw what a superb horse this was, of a fine character and responsive to my every movement.

An urge to ride in a swift canter swept through me. Now she showed me all her incredible power—and also her grace. Every movement was coordinated. She never tired, never broke her rhythm. My skin was burning from the wind. Grass and sky whirled about me. I looked up and saw the sun directly overhead. I decided I had better go back. Yankel was waiting for me on the road. I was afraid he would be angry at me for tiring the horse, but he waved his cap and shouted, "Hey, you ride just like a cossack." I was overjoyed.

Every night I worked at the tavern. I did my job as well as I could, but the only thing I thought about was the Arabian. I lived for the moment I could take her out and ride fast. The speed was voluptuous to me. For the first time in my life I realized how it felt to be free, and how constrained I had been before. When I came back from a ride covered with sweat, exhausted but happy, I thought with disgust how I used to sit studying all the time and did not even know if the sun was shining outside.

I did not contact the *rav*, or even my parents. I knew I should, but I delayed. Each day I told myself I would "tomorrow," and then tomorrow came and still I did not. I was busy running errands for Yankel. One time he sent me into the city. The moment I walked down the old, familiar streets, I was overwhelmed by grief, for everything brought back memories of Moishe. When I saw a student I knew from yeshiva coming toward me, I crossed over and hid myself in an alley. I leaned back against a wall and my heart was pounding hard. I could not bear the anguish of hearing anyone mentioning Moishe's name to me, nor did I want to be recognized. If word got around that I was in Kishinev, I would be pulled back to my old life, and I was not ready for that yet. I ran back to the tavern and wished I could have gone further away from Kishinev. Like a fugitive, I avoided going into the city again.

Yankel had a tobacco plantation in the countryside, and one day he told me he wanted me to accompany him there. I consented at once. Our journey began in the early morning and the weather was mild. We rode in a leisurely way beside a meandering brown river, a cloudless sky above, passing thatched cottages.

At one of these we stopped to get some water to drink. A dignified-looking peasant led us to his well where he had chained a bucket and cup for travelers to use. When Yankel tried to tip him, he refused. I saw that among the peasants could be found truly God-fearing men who were virtuous, even though they lacked the book learning of the rabbis in the city.

Our trip lasted about two hours longer. Yankel talked about his business, told me how much he disliked the tanners. "Such ruffians I would rather not meet. I wouldn't greet them on the street—but business is business." Meanwhile I looked around and the countryside reminded me of Cotu Mori. I felt refreshed and glad I was there.

Ahead we saw a very large house of white stucco, with columns and a veranda. Imagine my surprise when Yankel pulled up in front of it. For a moment I thought there must be some mistake.

A whole group of people rushed out to meet him, and they all went inside, with me following a distance behind. It was a thick-walled house with arched doorways. We went into a sitting room full of big, heavy furniture in dark colors, lamps with silk shades and fringes, tables covered with plush cloths, and potted plants. A turkish rug covered the floor and several were hung on the walls. Yankel's relatives gathered around him, and I stood to one side not knowing what to do. How should I act? Was I going to be treated as a servant in this house? Not until I saw all his luxurious possessions did I realize that Yankel was rich.

In order to occupy myself, I started staring at a portrait on the wall. It was of a slender, dark-eyed woman in a black satin dress. She sat at a small iron table in an orchard. On the table was a silver samovar, a cake stand with cakes, and a bowl of cherries. I studied every detail, the lines on the woman's face, her earrings, even the design on the table. A voice startled me.

"Is the subject so fascinating?"

I turned and it was as if the painting had come to life, but with a merrier expression. Neci, Yankel's wife, squeezed my arm. She whispered, "Don't be afraid here." Then more loudly she said, "David, come sit by my side."

She introduced Yankel's mother, Brena, and his brother and sister-in-law, Zalman and Frieda. Meanwhile she held my hand between hers and squeezed it affectionately.

"You should hear what a hero this boy is," Yankel said.

"A hero? What did he do?"

Yankel described the circumstances of our first meeting and all the hotel owner had told him about me. Everything was exaggerated in my favor and I was really embarrassed when he started boasting about what a saint and what a genius I was supposed to be.

Brena said, "Such a child you have snatched from his studies? You will have to give him several hours free every day so he can study."

"I agree, and no arguments," Neci added and gave my cheek a pinch.

I felt relaxed now. Although these people were wealthy, in a way they reminded me of those I had met at Mendel's hotel. Here also I was highly respected—no, revered—because I had attended a yeshiva. They delighted in singing my praises.

Zalman said, "I envy you, Yankel, you have someone to do your accounts."

His wife added, "Such a pious child will bring good fortune."

Yankel took me aside and told me, "I'm glad my wife likes you.

Since we don't have children, it's nice for her to have a young person around the house."

I was the center of attention, but not for long. Another guest arrived. Zalman's sixteen-year-old daughter, Sasa, a brunette with flashing black eyes, stepped into the room in high-heeled boots, her long skirt making a swishing sound.

"Good afternoon, Mother . . . good afternoon Aunt, Grandmother . . ."

Politely she made the rounds, and when she came to me I was blushing to meet this tall, beautiful girl. With her dimpled chin, she gave me only a curt nod.

Yankel began to repeat the story about me and Mendel to her, but it did not interest her much. In the middle she said, "Uncle, may I play?"

"Of course, why not, my darling?"

"What a treat, she never wants to play for us."

"Why today?"

Sasa did not seem to hear. She arranged herself at the piano, sitting erect, a severe expression on her face. Her neck was long, or so it seemed in the high-collared white blouse with pearl buttons she wore. Her hair was pinned up in a knot. She made me think of a swan.

For a few moments she held her pale, long-fingered hands above the keys, and I felt breathless and excited. The others did too. I could see how they looked at her adoringly. The old woman, Brena, had tears in her eyes as the music filled the room.

I had never heard this piece before, and yet it seemed to me she must have played it perfectly. Yet there was something that made me uncomfortable. Perhaps it was a stiffness, or a hardness in her playing—there was something I could not explain. When Sasa finished, she gave a little smile, and everyone praised her.

Neci announced that it was time to eat. We all got up, and on the way to the dining room I found myself walking beside Sasa. She rushed ahead to her uncle and said, "Does the hired hand have to sit with us when we have our meal?"

This really stung me. At the dinner, I took pains to remember all I had learned in the fine houses in Kishinev. I put a napkin on my lap; I was careful with the silver—not that anyone except Sasa seemed to be attentive to these details. For Yankel a knife was sufficient; he did not require a fork. Neci cooled her tea in a saucer. They all talked with their mouths full. For all my trouble I did not receive a single glance from Sasa.

I had never met anyone like this Sasa before. She was not rebuked for her insult to me. The family considered her higher than themselves. They were illiterate, but for Sasa the finest tutors had been hired, and she had had the education of an aristocrat's daughter—she wrote poetry, spoke several languages, and could paint. It was she who had painted the portrait of Neci. For all these accomplishments—and because Zalman and Frieda had only her, and Yankel and Neci had no child at all—she was treated like some holy object.

Every week Zalman brought his family for the Shabbes meal, and I had to endure the taunts and cold looks of this prideful girl. It seemed to amuse her if she could bring me to the point of tears. These visits were an ordeal to me. I was afraid to speak for fear that she would rudely interrupt me or burst into scornful laughter. What hurt most was when she did not notice me at all.

My first afternoon Yankel took me out to show me around. Never had I imagined anything like what I saw; it was more the estate of a nobleman than of a Jew. There were beautiful gardens and orchards of orange, lemon, and almond trees which happened to be in bloom. Bees buzzed everywhere. The air was sweet and fragrant. In the vineyards the pruned plants had begun to put out green leaves. Birds perched on the trellis as if awaiting the juicy grapes. Close by was the wine warehouse. We went inside, and it was cool as we walked through the rooms and Yankel showed me the enormous casks where the wine was stored. A sour smell came from the ones where wine was still fermenting.

Finally we rode out to the tobacco fields. All over were peasants setting plants into the newly ploughed, rich black earth. I tried to count how many workers there were, but so many did I see that their faces began to blur. I could only estimate that there were

more than a hundred. Yankel told me that my main job was going to
be recording how much each person worked and how much was
owed in wages.

The next day I returned and brought a book with blank pages
with me. The Russian foreman refused to speak to me and would
not answer my questions. I went to the other workers and addressed them respectfully, and they explained to me how everything was done. Only when the foreman saw me writing things
down in the notebook did he come rushing over to me. "What are
you doing? I figure everything out in my head."

I said, "'From now on I write things down."

In the afternoon the foreman was not at work and I was told he
went to consult with the priest. It was a little before twilight when
he returned. He came over to me, this time with a friendlier manner. "I understand you have attended a yeshiva. Then you must be
intelligent and can understand what I say. I am paid four rubles a
week. I get up when God sleeps and work until evening. What
does it hurt if we take something extra? The boss is a rich man." I
did not know what words to answer him, but the expression on my
face served instead to show him I was not agreeable to his plan. He
begged me not to mention this to Yankel and I promised.

I was troubled by what he told me. Perhaps the man deserved
more money. I could not decide what to do, but finally that night I
blurted out to Yankel, "Can you raise the foreman's salary?"

Yankel became angry. "What? Raise his salary? He works only
for the season and I pay him the entire year. So why should I give
him more?"

After this I tried to avoid the foreman, but if I did have dealings
with him I showed him a certain deference, just as I did the workers. I was inexperienced and they knew what they were doing. I
tried to learn everything I could from them about tobacco. It
seems it was a fragile and risky crop. If there was a hailstorm, the
pellets went right through the thin leaves and they could not be
sold as cigar wrappers. The plants easily became diseased. Small
green worms, the same color as the leaves they fed on, were a nui-
sance, and the workers were always busy picking them off. About

every third season some disaster occurred and Yankel lost the whole crop, but the price he could get when it grew undamaged was so high that it made up for all losses.

The day arrived when I had to distribute the wages. I consulted my account book and kept strictly to it. It took several hours to pay everyone. In the end there was a lot of money left over beyond the usual amount Yankel gave for wages. The foreman disappeared again because he knew I was going to return the extra money. Yankel was furious and so distrustful of all the workers when he saw the foreman had been robbing him, that he said, "I would rather have a fifteen-year-old Jew than a goy." He put me in the foreman's place.

That I was promoted to this position made a difference in my whole manner. I felt I had some importance in this world and that possibly I had a fine future ahead of me. Even when I met Sasa I was more confident. For the first time I could look at her without turning red, and I even dared to say a few words. Once she and her parents were visiting and Yankel started boasting that I was a scholar. This Sasa could not tolerate. She decided to say something to me in Russian, thinking I would not understand and she would humiliate me before her relations. I answered her well with a quip both in Russian and yiddish so the others could laugh with me. "He must be clever," her father said, "if he can answer Sasa back." Begrudgingly she came over later and said, "I thought you were ignorant like everyone else here. But it appears you are not. What have you read? Have you read Tolstoy?" I said no. Then she asked if I had read Pushkin. I said I had read several works by him in Yiddish.

Her compliments did not turn my head. I knew how haughty Sasa was. Her parents were trying to marry her off. In each prospective bridegroom, Sasa managed to find a fault. One was ugly, another did not speak well, and yet another was stupid. Frieda went to synagogue to pray the right one would be found. Yankel made large contributions to charity in honor of his niece so the Creator might be persuaded to help, and Zalman traveled from matchmaker to matchmaker. He offered fifteen thousand rubles as dowry and *kest* for life—and he would have offered it into eternity if that were possible.

Once Neci said to me, "What do you think of Sasa?" My reply was "Nothing, of course. I have the Arabian. Why should I think of girls?" This reassured her. I knew that as far as they were concerned, Sasa was way above me.

As foreman, my work was a struggle. The peasants resisted me. How could they stand to work under such a young boy and a "Yid" besides. Several complained to their priest and he comforted them. Others quit. I saw it did not matter; I could find plenty to replace them. I began to understand that the peasants needed to please me to get their bread, and I felt more authority.

There were many workers who could not convince themselves of my honesty, and they urged me to apply the old system of cheating. I wondered why they could not believe in a pure person. I always walked away when they made improper suggestions, and yet they continued to make them. Little by little they wanted to wear me down.

One of them, an old man named Ivan, came up to me while I was resting in the shade of a tree and eating a snack.

"Forgive me, sir, shall I keep you company?"

"Why not?"

"Forgive me asking, where do you come from?"

I told him, and he answered that he had lived in that area when he was a young man and worked in the wheat fields.

"I remember there was a government official who had built a wheat silo in the middle of this big field. The workers made a tunnel beneath it and took out a few sacks of grain a night. The thefts were so gradual that they were unnoticed until there was almost nothing left."

You see, sir, I'm just an ignorant man, but there's a great lesson in that story. Everything gets worn away little by little. I've seen water cut a gap in a rock. There's no sense thinking you're stronger than a rock."

"I'm not a rock, I'm a man, and I try to live honestly."

"People should take pleasure whenever they can. I've lived a long life and that's what I learned."

When he parted from me, I thought about his words and understood his meaning well. I was certain the workers could not wear me away and make me dishonest under any conditions—not even if Neci and Yankel were not as kind to me as they were.

As pious as I believed myself to be, I still had not bothered to write my parents and inform them where I was. I told myself I was saving my wages and then I would send them a large sum of money and surprise them. The truth was I was afraid that they would make me come home and give up everything. One time when I was feeling guilty, I confessed to Neci. I expected her to reprimand me, but instead she started to laugh. "Look how big he is; at his age my father was married and had a child, but this one wants to suckle his mother's breasts." After this, whenever she saw me downcast she would taunt me with this, and she could not have said anything which disturbed me more. I wanted everyone to consider me a man, not a boy.

When I had been working as foreman several weeks, Yankel came to me and suggested the workers might accept me better if I put aside my orthodox clothes. Inside I felt shocked, but I covered over my feelings and said I agreed to change my clothes. I did not want Yankel to think I lacked ambition to succeed. Also a part of me was pleased with the idea of changing my appearance, of visibly distinguishing myself from the boy I had been before.

Soon after I talked to Yankel a tailor came to take my measurements. In two weeks he returned, not just with a suit, but a new shirt, underwear, and other things. Everything was laid out on my bed waiting. There was a peaked hat, a short jacket, trousers, boots, a tie, and a Russian-style shirt with a round neck with a stand-up collar and embroidery in red thread down the front. Neci insisted I bathe, and she herself washed my hair in wine. To me these preparations made it seem like a holy day.

Then I went to get dressed. There was a small mirror in my room. When I looked at myself in these new clothes, I got really frightened. If I had appeared in Shumsk dressed as I now looked, I would have been driven from the town and mourned by my parents. Had I not witnessed the case of Gershon and Feiga? Instead of being called by their fathers' names as was customary, the husband was called Feiga's Gershon and the wife Gershon's Feiga, as if they belonged only to each other. The reason for this was that the wife did not wear a *shaytl* and the husband had a trimmed beard, cut *peyes*, and a short jacket. Everyone avoided them. When a feebleness descended on the small children of Shumsk it was believed to be caused by the grave sins of this couple. They were forced to flee.

Then I began to think bitterly of my previous poverty, and I accepted my appearance. It seemed to me the important thing was to show proper gratitude. I came into the next room where Yankel and Neci awaited me. I kissed their hands and they kissed me on the forehead. Neci said, "You shall not lack as long as I am alive."

A short while after, on an impulse, I cut off my long *peyes*. Somehow I survived this too. I did not even feel too bad about it.

More and more I cut myself off from my old life, and a profound change began to take place in me. I stopped studying. I shortened my morning prayers until I scarcely prayed at all. The yeshiva, I heard, had reopened, but did I care? It had nothing to do with me. Yankel's estate was the only home I knew, and it was a Garden of Eden with earthly pleasures.

I, the sober boy, whose body used to ache and whose eyes had been going blind from constant study, became a prankster. Sometimes people were really hurt by my mischief, but they were not aware I was the culprit, and I felt no guilt. A carpenter's son in Shumsk had once taught me a trick, how to drill a hole in a wall and insert a needle which I could pull with a thread and give someone a painful prick. In Shumsk I had not paid attention. Now the boy's precise instructions came back and it seemed delightful to me to practice this at the Shabbes services.

Better than anywhere else, I loved to play tricks at the *Shul.* Once I hid behind the pulpit when the women were praying. I changed my voice and spoke to them so that it seemed God's voice was coming from the altar. Innocent as they were, they did not think to inspect the hiding place where I was rolling around and holding in the laughter. In their imagination it was not possible that anyone would desecrate the holiness of the *shul.* So they believed that a miracle had occurred. I did feel a little regret when I saw them telling people of this event and I saw they were making fools of themselves. What if the truth were discovered and Neci, who always treated me lovingly, was humiliated? I thought of the saying, "It's a fool who throws a stone into a garden and then ten wise, good people cannot dig it out." But I never let myself be weighed down with self-accusations.

The next week I simply went to the *shul* with Yankel and we sat in the front in the best seats. And who looked around to see if anyone was crying at the services? Rich people do not cry, only the beggars who sit in the back do.

Nearly always I was lighthearted. People would say to Yankel and Neci, "It's merry in your house. It's never depressed. We wish it was so good at our place. What's the secret of all this happiness?"

I saw that the more pranks I played, the better they liked me. Neci would have to run over and cover my mouth with her hand and shout, "Be quiet, fresh one, or I'll slap your cheeks." Immediately I mimicked her. She would grab the broom and chase me, and I would scamper about the room just out of her reach. When I was tired of the joke I would run out, jump on my Arabian, and ride away for a few hours.

Every spare moment I was racing the horse, and I was not as gentle to her as at the beginning. I would risk my life in these rides. If there was a fence, it had to be jumped. If there was a cliff, I had to ride along the edge. People adopted Yankel's nickname for me: "the Cossack."

A certain hardness even came into the way I acted. When I was at work ordering the peasants about, I was able to make people afraid. I experienced the sweetness of power. And now the workers accepted me because in my clothes and in the way I acted, I was not like a Jew.

One day I had a surprise while working at the wine warehouse doing an inventory. Yankel came in with his niece and asked me to walk her home. We walked along and Sasa was talkative. She started to praise me for no longer wearing orthodox clothes, and for being "modern." I was a little astonished to hear this kind of rhetoric from her. Suddenly I noticed some cavalry soldiers in the distance. I watched them come down the road and past us and completely forgot about my companion for the moment.

Sasa got insulted. She said, "Look at how he gapes at a horse when he has a girl at his side." The next thing I saw, she had stopped walking and refused to go on.

"Come on, I have to get back to work," I said.

"I'll give you what you want," she answered.

"What's that?"

"A kiss."

"Give it," I said, without a moment's hesitation, although my heart was pounding. Her lips burned my cheek. We walked to her house in silence. I had sinned, and not just with my eyes—but I was trembling with joy.

The kiss was all I needed to make my imagination soar. In my fantasies I was like Joseph who had gone into Egypt and risen to a position of great power. After all, why shouldn't I marry into a rich family? Earlier it had seemed impossible, but not now. All other bridegrooms had been unacceptable to Sasa. My mind began calculating, going over the dowry, and the bride as well. Suddenly I worshiped Sasa. She was a beauty, refined and intelligent. Whatever she lacked, I imagined she had, and the pledge of her kiss convinced me she cared for me.

The only difficulty was that I was still affianced to Perl. It was painful to think of these two girls together, when one was so exalted to me and the other so low. I said to Yankel one morning, "Do you think it's possible for a person to get out of a betrothal?" When he answered, "As long as no plates have been broken, and better can be found," I rejoiced.

A week and a half passed. I was working in the tobacco fields. The plants were full-grown now, and soon the workers were going to pick the leaves and spread them out to dry. A servant came up to me and asked me to go over to a more secluded spot so he could give me a message. We did so, and he handed me a note from Sasa.

It said she wanted me to meet her at her aunt Zelda's house the following Saturday. As soon as I had the opportunity I wrote a note and sent it to her, that she should expect me.

To me it was almost an eternity until the day arrived. Just as I was about to leave, Brena came to the house and she said she wanted me to come to her home for Shabbes. Neci said, "David is mine. I'm not giving him anywhere," and the two women began to bicker. One pulled my left arm and the other, my right. I broke away from them and ran out. Neci came to the door and screamed, "Where are you going?"

"To *Shul.*"

"Since when did you get so religious?"

I knew she was really angry. It did not matter. I was going to do anything necessary in order to see Sasa, even if it meant deceiving people.

I walked along at a good pace and soon I came to Sasa's aunt's. Zelda, a fat widow with rosy cheeks, opened the door and recognized me. *"Gut Shabbes,"** she said cheerfully, "but what are you doing here? Sasa's here too. Is there something going on between the two of you?" I started laughing and told her not to worry. She led me to her sitting room where Sasa was waiting.

It was not just Sasa, but a whole crowd, three other young men and two women. I was crushed. I expected a more private visit, but Sasa gave me a radiant smile and that comforted me. Aunt Zelda said, "Well, children, I will leave you to enjoy yourselves and sing Shabbes hymns," and she left.

As soon as she was gone, one of the girls said, "Can we talk in front of him?" I looked around and finally realized she meant me. Sasa assured her I was "safe." Then a young man with blond hair and a German accent got up and said, "What are we going to do with the bloodhound?"

"You mean the inspector from the fourth ward?" Sasa asked.

"Yes, he's killing us out, searching our comrades, and arresting right and left."

Gradually I began to understand what it was about, and I was

* Good Sabbath.

disgusted. This was a revolutionary group and they were planning how they were going to kill the police inspector. What kind of company was this for Sasa? Did she understand, for instance, who the ruffian in the corner was—one Froike, a tanner I remembered from the tavern where I had worked as a waiter. He was considered, even in that environment, a vicious person.

Sasa and the others made a fuss over him because he had "committed himself to clearing the path." That meant when the explosives were obtained, he was the one who was going to throw the bomb.

The whole time I said nothing. I waited until the end because I wanted to speak to Sasa alone and ask her why she was endangering her aunt. One by one they left, and the last one to go was Froike.

When we were alone I asked, "Why did you invite me?"

"I thought you'd want to join us; Froike needs help."

"That's impossible. . . . Tell me, how can you do this to your aunt?"

"No one will suspect her. That's why it's safe, and Aunt Zelda is too stupid to suspect us."

When I heard these words I understood that just the way Sasa used her aunt, she used others. Her friendliness, and even the kiss, came about only because she wanted to involve me in her plot. I said, "I'm going." She got frightened and asked me if I was going to tell, and I answered no.

My mood was completely subdued from what it had been on the way to this meeting. I walked home with bent head. Not only had I lost Sasa, but I was depressed that I could not escape these underground groups. Everywhere was someone ready to commit an assassination. Maybe Sasa's group would not succeed, because the people I met that afternoon seemed fonder of making long speeches than acting.

As I approached the house I felt contrite about how I had run off and left Neci earlier. Probably it was because I was capable of such acts that Sasa considered me a candidate for her gang. I went inside and apologized to Neci. She said she would forgive me, but I saw she was still angry. What irritated her the most was that I went to sit by myself in a sad mood. At dinner I could not eat anything. Instead I went out for a walk in the fields.

There was a big, red moon. The tobacco rose around me, ready to be picked. I ran my fingers over the sticky leaves. The pungent tobacco odor rose to my nose.

I was surprised to see people ahead. I thought no one was around but me, but there was a man and woman. I heard a gay laugh I thought I recognized. I began to follow the couple and made little noise, except for the rustle of the leaves. Suddenly the two seemed to disappear. I went to the spot where I had last seen them.

Froike had spread out his coat on the ground. Sasa lay upon it and they were fornicating like animals.

I felt sickened by them, but more by myself. In that moment I saw clearly how far I had wandered from the path of righteousness. Soon I, too, would become bestial. There was not that much difference between Froike and myself.

I went back to the house, stopped at the well, and poured bucket after bucket of water over my head, but still I did not feel clean.

I felt I should go home to my parents, but the temptations the plantation presented were too great for me. I had become a weak person who could not live without being surrounded by comforts. No matter how I struggled, I could not leave.

Then something happened. Trouble descended on Neci and Yankel and all Jews who lived in the vicinity, and it seemed wrong to leave them at this time.

A Jewish neighbor, Shulim, had hired a Russian servant, who became pregnant. Immediately the girl was sent home. She told her father her employer was responsible for her condition. He took the matter to court and Shulim was subpoenaed.

Perhaps the whole thing could have been kept quiet, but the local priest made it the subject of every sermon. He pictured Jews to his congregants as greedy and evil lechers. He said, "The Egyptians understood how Jews should be treated. They quartered them, and we should do the same." It seems this priest had a private quarrel with Shulim. The priest had borrowed five hundred rubles which he had not paid back, and suddenly he insisted that it was a two-hundred-ruble loan and the rest was interest which he refused to pay. His sermons caused such outrage among the peasants that it became clear that when the trial took place, if a verdict of guilty was entered, Jewish blood would be shed copiously.

Up to and on the day of the trial, Shulim was calm. He had been to the Bahotz rabbi, to whom he had sworn he was innocent. The rabbi told him the truth would be revealed at the trial. Russians and Jews filled the courtroom. A judge sat in front, one who said publicly that he hated all Jews and that he held them guilty of killing Christ—so how would he judge Shulim now that he had him in his hands? When the servant girl entered the court with her swollen stomach, it created a sensation. The judge had to call for order as she walked slowly forward. Everyone was solicitous of her. The prosecutor treated her so gently that truly it was he who testified in her place. When the defense attorney rose and got ready to cross-examine her, the judge became furious. He said, "Is it necessary to torment the poor child when it is clear already what happened and who was at fault?" Shulim's lawyer would have had to sit down, but the girl herself spoke up and said, "I don't mind a few questions." So she was cross-examined. Throughout, she maintained Shulim was the father.

The lawyer saw it was futile, so he turned from her and addressed the court. "Honorable judge. The Jew has transgressed and will have to be punished in the prescribed way. He deserves it. Everything must be done according to the law. We must also consider that he still has certain rights. We are all agreed that the child is his. When it is born, the Jew has the right to circumcise a male child and give it a Jewish name."

When the girl heard these words her face became red. "What do you mean? I am carrying a holy child in my womb from a messenger of God. Do you think I will allow this child to become a Jew?"

The judge immediately tried to quiet her. "Even if it were a

Jewish child you are giving birth to, you could do with it whatever you felt like. You could bring it into the church, so don't be afraid."

The prosecutor went up to her and said sternly, "I warn you, if you retract your story, that means you swore falsely. It's against the law and you will be punished."

The girl was still excited and did not consider what she was saying. She blurted out, "If I have the honor to carry the priest's child, I don't see why I shouldn't tell the truth. Why should I have people think I was whore to a Jew?" Then she told how she had gone to confess before the priest and he had promised her that he would elevate her to becoming the Holy Mary. He gave her directions as to where they should meet. Being a religious girl, she had obeyed him. When she informed him she had become pregnant, the priest made her promise that she would say that the Jew she worked for was the father. When she finished this story, she burst into tears.

The judge declared the case dismissed.

That night all the Jews gathered at Yankel's to rejoice in the miracle of the Bahotz rabbi. Yankel took out a heavy silver tray and spread layers of money over it. This was placed by the door, and anyone who came in was invited to take a present. The furniture was pushed back against the walls to make a larger space. The tables were covered with linen, and pitchers of wine were set out along with trays of fish, cheese, fruit, and bread. All who tasted the wine declared that it was *vermerazik.* °

Everyone came; no one could hold back from this celebration. Even Sasa and her crowd arrived, and I could see them whispering together merrily and trying to decide whether to assassinate this one or that one. All around people were dancing and singing, but not me. When I saw Sasa I thought how I should have returned to Shumsk. My poor parents did not know if I was alive. I started drinking wine, not to celebrate the victory, but to ease my heart.

° A Purim wine, referred to in the Bible, which was so fine that it "made the heart of a king light."

Yankel came over to me and said, "David, go down to the cellar and get a barrel more of that *vermerazik.*"

I took a lantern and began to descend the cellar steps. I was careless. Where the ceiling was low, I forgot to bend down. Suddenly my head smashed hard against a beam. I dropped the lantern and tumbled down the stairs and lay at the bottom unconscious.

The next thing I knew I was in my room, my head was bandaged, and a strange woman all in white sat in a chair beside me. When she saw I was awake, she called Neci. Neci said, "David, do you know who I am?"

"Of course I know who you are, but I don't know who this woman is."

"This is a nurse. Don't you realize you are hurt?"

"The only thing I know is that I have a terrible headache."

She explained to me that when I did not come back with the wine, Yankel thought I was tippling by myself in the cellar. He and several others came to look for me and found me with my feet and body on the steps and my head on the ground in a pool of blood. They carried me upstairs and sent for a doctor. This was two weeks ago, and I had been unconscious ever since.

A doctor came later in the day to examine the stitches I had received and to rebandage my head. He said I had to lie quietly a few more days.

They left me alone with the nurse. Immediately her head fell on her chest and she snored. I tried to get up but found I could not; if I lifted myself only a little, my head started to reel. I thirsted for water and my head throbbed.

I had received a terrible blow—and it was just this blow I needed to fully awaken all my remorse. I had to lie there helpless, but I wanted to get up and go to Shumsk to my parents. Every moment my head pounded as if a hammer were striking it, but I felt I deserved punishment. I should have been struck down even harder.

In a few days I was permitted to walk about by myself and receive visitors. Yankel, Zalman, and many neighbors visited with me. They told me they had prayed for me. I said, "I am not worthy of your prayers. I abandoned my parents."

"Is this David talking? You are not yourself."

Gradually I healed, but the loneliness and longing I felt for my parents did not leave me. I was never happy anymore. I did not joke and I played no pranks. I began to cry all the time. People tried to comfort me, but it did not help.

One day Neci said, "You want to go home. Wait another week until I am certain you are healthy and then you will be gone. There will be an end to this crying. After you satiate yourself with your parents, you can return."

Just as she promised, at the end of the week, she gave me a suitcase and I packed.

⁓6

I lose three mothers

SHUMSK AND ZAKIT, 1891–1892

I HATE TO SAY how much time I was on the plantation. By the time
I left, it was the end of the summer of 1891. I was sixteen years old.
My parents had not seen me since my fourteenth birthday.

It was not a servant who took me to the train station, but Yankel
himself. The whole time we rode along in the wagon, I longed for
him to tell me not to leave, but as if from spite he would not make
a sign. He talked a lot in his usual loud way, pointed to the fallow
fields we passed, and made observations about the excellent crop
we had had that summer. Just before I got on the train, he gave me
one hundred rubles and said I should hide it carefully. Surprised
by his generosity, I tied the money in my handkerchief and slipped
it inside my shirt. Suddenly serious, Yankel clasped me in his arms
tightly, and then without a word we parted.

My seat was by the window, and I stuffed my luggage beneath.
As the train began to move, I caught a last glimpse of Yankel
standing by a pillar. I started banging on the glass and waving; he
saw me, but was motionless. The train picked up speed and he
disappeared from my sight.

Once again I was in the countryside traveling from one distant
part of Russia to another. The landscape became increasingly severe. I could not take my eyes from the bare earth, but soon a wet,

gray mist blotted out everything. I started shivering; I felt as if the mist were going inside me. A peasant next to me offered me a drink, a fiery brew and that helped a little.

I got off at a town called Chernyy Ostrov because I had an uncle there. From Uncle Yossel I got a stern reprimand about my appearance and had to stay a few weeks to exchange my clothes for orthodox garb and let my *peyes* grow. My uncle's wife, Zipporah, had reverted to childhood. She sat all day in a broken rocking chair, giggling and hugging herself. I could hardly bear to be with her. I had to give her mush for lunch, and it would drool down her chin. I left one day without a word and took a train to Shumsk. So my *peyes* were a little short.

The weather gave me a dismal welcome. It was raining in torrents. The street was mud and it splattered over me as I went to my house. I slipped inside, chilled to the bone, and there all my family was gathered except my father. It frightened me that my mother was wearing a black apron. I went up to her. The color drained from her face and she swooned. My grandmother started to shriek in such a way that I understood she had become fairly senile. At the same time my two youngest brothers began to cry loudly. One shouted, "Go away," and the other, "Please don't hurt us." So much noise came from our house that several neighbors came rushing in.

Soon my father arrived. I ran over to him and tried to hug him. He pushed me away coldly and this hurt me. Without thinking I took out the money I had and offered it to him. He said, "I don't expect anything from you." All this happened quickly. He rushed to my mother and tried to bring her around.

The only one who kept calm was my sister Hindah. In the last year she had taken on the responsibility of visiting the sick and dying, both Jews and goyim. She had learned to control her feelings in the most dire situations. Now she went about and politely asked neighbors to leave, and made herself useful with the children and with my grandmother, whom she took into the other room.

Meanwhile my mother gained consciousness and called me to

her. She clasped my hands so tightly that she hurt me. It turned out that she had been in mourning for me! When she and the others saw me, they must have thought I had risen from the dead. I saw my mother was weak, that she had been sick, that she looked like an old woman—grief had robbed her of her health. It was a struggle for her to speak. She glanced heavenward and said, "Lord, don't let the pain my child has caused me count as his sins." Her words wounded me more than my father's.

It was a bitter reception I received in Shumsk. I could not walk through the town without people giving me dark looks. Everyone blamed me and considered me sinful. Even the most wretched person was higher than me, and in my own mind, this was true also. All my accomplishments in Bessarabia seemed like nothing.

I kept thinking I was supposed to get married, but during this time no one said anything and I never saw Perl or Bracha, as if those two had never existed. Instead it turned out my sister was going to get married. It was a real struggle for us to prepare for the wedding. Even a pauper was not excused from providing his daughter with a dowry. The money I could contribute would help only a little. We decided to appeal to an uncle in Dubnow, Nutah Toback. I wrote the letter myself and truly labored over it. Each word I weighed and reweighed before I set it down, so that my sister's fate would not be determined by some carelessness on my part. If we did not get the funds, the match would be called off and Hindah would remain a spinster. I finished and then decided to include, on some separate pages, the following story which I had learned from my teacher at yeshiva. I thought it would plead my cause better than I could.

"There was once a rich and well-educated man named Shmuel Faivel. He sat up day and night incessantly studying. The slightest noise disturbed him and made him ill-tempered. He decided to instruct his wife and children never to talk to him. Even this was not enough. He had to build a special study in the back of his house, apart from everyone. The only contact he had with people was when his wife brought him a tray of food.

"In this manner, for many years, he sat alone and read volume after volume. He began to age. Intuitively he knew that his death would come soon, and he made out a will. It stipulated that his children would inherit his wealth on one condition: they had to provide his coffin with candles so that when he arrived in Heaven he could sit and study and pursue his greatest pleasure.

"Shmuel Faivel died. He had left an enormous fortune, and his children felt they did not have to stint on a box of candles. They provided him with the best paraffin ones they could buy.

"Shmuel Faivel arrived in Heaven and was about to sit down and study. He tried to light one of his candles when he realized that he did not have a match. He became frantic. Because of one small object, a match, he had lost everything. He wandered about in darkness with a feeling of distress, when suddenly he saw a light in the distance. He ran toward it and to his astonishment he recognized a familiar visage. It was Moishe Chaim, his water carrier.

"He cried out, 'Moishe Chaim.'

"At first the water carrier could not see him.

" 'Can't you recognize the voice of Shmuel Faivel for whom you carried water so many years?'

" 'Yes, yes, now I recognize. What do you want, Harav Shmuel Faivel?'

"So he said, 'Listen to me, where can I get a match? Candles I have a full box, but I forgot to bring matches and I see that you have a light, so I believe you must have some matches. Please give me a few.'

"Moishe Chaim replied, 'Don't you understand, Harav Shmuel Faivel, that in Heaven one doesn't create light by lighting a candle? He who makes other people's lives lighter with his money and by caring for them while he is alive, fulfills the law of Talmud.

" 'A man eats the fruits in the world and the seed is sprouted in the coming world—but not by bringing along a box of candles in a coffin.' "

With great hope we sent this letter out, and with rejoicing we received the reply. Uncle Nutah said that he enjoyed the story. He telegraphed us a considerable sum. My sister would marry an excellent groom, a young man known for his good character and the grandson of a rabbi.

With the money my parents gave a lavish wedding. It went on for seven full days and consumed every kopeck we received from my uncle. Everyone came to witness the marriage of a virtuous Jewish daughter, even my relatives from Proskurov.

People were astonished when an elegant coach arrived. The driver jumped down to open the door, and out stepped Uncle Nuchem and Aunt Bobbah. My uncle wore a new and expensive suit and my aunt had adorned herself in a fantastic manner with peacock feathers, silks, and glittering jewels. She took her husband's arm, which he had to raise up a little, since he was considerably shorter, and they strolled among the other guests with a dignified manner, my aunt taking the opportunity to scrutinize everything with a critical air. People made way for this stylish pair.

When my aunt noticed me, she stopped her promenade. I stared at her attire and she at mine. I suppose she was wondering how I had managed to get a decent pair of boots, and it disturbed her. She addressed me in a loud voice so all the guests could hear: "Look at my great friend. He lived at my house, took everything, and what gratitude did he show? He never even wrote a letter."

And I screamed back, "How could I write when the fare from Proskurov cost seven and a half rubles and I only had five."

A little later my uncle came up to me with a sheepish manner. "David, I'm sorry. If I had known it cost more, I would have given you the extra money." He began to apologize so fervently that I forgave him. Anyway, it was my sister's wedding and it was impossible to hold a grudge on such a day.

Generally a brother is happy when a sister marries, but I was ecstatic. Hindah and I had always been close. We had suffered together under our old tutors, and as the older one, she gave me comfort then and later when the changes in my father's fortune made our lives hard. While I was away, because of my mother's sickness, she had taken on most of the household duties. I saw she had grown into a gentle, good person.

At the wedding feast I was so merry and full of pranks that my parents need not have hired a jester. I amused all our guests; even Aunt Bobbah forsook her sour exprssion and laughed. I was among the young men who hoisted the bridegroom into the air and danced round with him. I ate, drank, sang, forgot all sad thoughts.

During the feast my brother Beryl came and told me someone wanted to speak to me. I followed him outside. Down the street I saw a figure completely in black. My hair stood up on end. To my drunken senses, it was like the Angel of Death. In a moment I was sober. As I went closer I saw it was a woman wearing a *shaytl*. I was astonished. It was Perl.

"Who put that wig on your head?"

"An eighty-year-old grocer from Alik."

I was ashamed to even look at her. When I saw her last she looked like a child. Now she looked like a shrivelled old woman, thinner than ever. I knew I had disgraced Perl. People always suspected there was something wrong with a bride who was abandoned. I tried to say something cheerful. "Well, it's lucky you got married while your mother is still alive."

"She's dead."

The music from the wedding came from the distance and the sound of laughter, and meanwhile Perl cried bitterly. She took out a white handkerchief and twisted it over and over as if it would help her to get control of herself. Finally she said brokenly, "Wish your . . . sister a happy . . . life. . . ." She lingered a few more moments, staring at the ground, and I did too. Then with a long, sad sigh she turned, and I looked up to watch her walk away from me with her frail shoulders all hunched.

It took me a long time before I felt able to return to the celebration. When I did, my mother came rushing up to me and rebuked me that I had been away. I said, "I saw Perl." She started questioning me about the meeting and was furious that Perl had dared to talk to me. Bracha had been against the marriage to the grocer and Perl had married without permission, and for this reason everyone blamed Perl for her mother's death. She had brought her mother great sorrow. No one in Shumsk would talk to Perl or gave her any pity.

* * *

After the wedding, we had nine people in the household, plus a groom living on *kest*. The struggle for existence resumed. Once again my father was running around begging people to let him do some chores for them, anything to make a kopeck. Now my mother had leisure to remember the pain I had caused her while I was away. She brooded on this continually and nothing could distract her.

Two months passed. One day I came home and she waved a letter in my face. It had arrived earlier but she had been waiting for a moment when everyone but we two was out of the house before she gave it to me. Meanwhile she had worked herself up to a terrible state. She screamed at me, "What whore writes you? What disgusting brothel were you in?" I became confused. I did not know what she was talking about. Tears streamed down her cheeks and she continued to make these accusations. I snatched the letter from her hand and read it quickly: "Beloved child, we all miss you, even the Arabian. Please return. Just telegraph and we will send you money for your fare. Yours, Neci." What harm was there in this letter? A bitter feeling came over me. I said, "Please don't call someone who has been like a mother to me, a whore."

This had a terrible effect. "Beloved one! Let me scratch your eyes, then maybe you will see." My mother flung herself on me and began scratching my face. She had become so thin that she had little strength, but even so she was in such a frenzy that it was hard to hold her still. She was gasping and I was terrified she would choke. While I struggled with her, I screamed for help loudly.

Fortunately Hindah came in now. She ran up to us and put her arms around my mother from behind and started talking to her. My sister's touch was magical. Suddenly my mother turned around and collapsed in Hindah's arms. "Look what he has driven me to. Good God, what have I done?" Hindah led her to the bed and had her lay down. I saw that my help was not needed; there was nothing I could do for my mother.

Unwilling to stay in the house another moment, I ran out. I

walked along the street with my head down, not greeting anyone I passed. Since my return I had held my feelings back, but now they flooded my heart. I despised Shumsk. Everything, even the small town accents, grated on me. What kind of future did I have here? Could I rise in the world? Even my boyhood friends had left. Shmuel was studying to be a scribe, and Gur Aryeh had married and moved to a city. Simcha Godels had left too.

I started thinking about how I used to go to study with Alter Richels. I had seen him at the Bes Medresh but I avoided him because I was afraid he would lecture me on my bad behavior. Now suddenly I longed to talk to him.

I went running through the streets until I came to his house. I was glad that there was a candle burning in his study. I could go in there by a separate door and did not have to encounter the rest of the household. I knocked and a voice called, "Please come in."

Alter Richels seemed older and weaker than I remembered or than he had appeared at a distance. He did not look at me sternly, but smiled in sincere welcome. He came over and embraced me warmly. Nothing could have made me feel worse for neglecting him. I kissed his hand and said, "Please forgive me for not coming to see you until now."

We sat down together, and suddenly I felt calmer. There was a samovar bubbling on a table behind us, and Alter Richels asked me to get two cups of tea. I drank my tea gratefully, but I saw he left his untouched. We started to read together, as we used to do. In the middle of a page I could hold back no longer and said, "I have something to tell you. I think I'm going to run away and go to Bessarabia."

Everything this man did was with a quiet thoughtfulness, and he considered my words for a long time. Absently his hand stroked his long beard.

"One can never tell what fortune will come to an individual. It's best to be patient. Your mother's health is poor, and how will you feel if you are responsible for making her sicker? If you can, try to stay just a little longer and see what happens."

I burst out, "I'm idle. I loaf around and am useless. I could endure, I could be patient, if I had work. On the tobacco plantation where I was, I was busy every second."

He tooked tired when he answered me, as if my visit had exhausted him. "You have my promise you shall have work." He stood up, and I knew our interview was over.

A few days later I found a place where I could be alone and wrote an answer to Neci, because such a kind person must not be ignored. I addressed her in the same manner she had me, and wrote: "Beloved mother, I fear that we will only see one another in our fantasies, or maybe in a dream—but not in reality." I was truly blind in not seeing to whom I was addressing these words.

Almost immediately I had the chance of a job. It was as a tutor in Zakit, a nearby village. Alter Richel's recommendation had gotten me excellent terms—forty rubles a term instead of the usual twenty-five. My future employer had consulted only my father, and my father, without asking my mother or me, had signed the contract. When he came and informed us, my mother became hysterical and pleaded with him not to take me from her again. But my father was adamant. He was afraid we would starve, so how could he give up the extra salary?

I don't know how I was so heartless not to see the extent of my mother's suffering. All of her arguments irritated me and made me want to get away all the more. I would not let myself notice how her hands trembled, how distractedly her eyes wandered about the room, then suddenly a look of pain crossed her features as she remembered we would be parted. I avoided her when I could, but even so she found an occasion to get me alone and inform me, "If you go, you won't see me alive."

"Why are you torturing me? I have no choice. Father signed the contract—anyway, it's not so far."

I left that Sunday.

Zakit was in the center of a forest. The trees were thick and tall, the ground covered with moss, pine needles, and dead branches. It was a gloomy place. A few wood cabins—that's all.

My employer's house was built like a small fortress. There were tiny windows into which scarcely any light could enter, and a low ceiling. It was called a "black house" because there was no proper chimney, only a few holes in the roof. The walls were all stained black, and the atmosphere inside was choking. The house was four hundred years old, and this was amazing because wood cottages like this usually burned down after a few years. In front of the house was a gate with a very low arch. Anyone who came to visit had to bend to get under and in this way they expressed respect. But I had another interpretation, that this was a sign of the oppression of living in such a place. To think I had spent my childhood in such villages and been happy!

There were six in the househld—Yeshovua Greenshpan and his wife, an elderly grandmother, and three children. My students were Chaim, Asher, and Rayzel. I started teaching them Hebrew, arithmetic, writing, and Russian. I sat at a rough wooden table and they sat on the floor. Yeshovua's wife would bustle around cooking. Clothes were strewn over bars and beams. My eyes teared from the smoky stove. At night I sat by the stove and read the few books I had brought with me; I had carried them all the way from Kishinev, and by this time they were falling apart. The lamp I read by consisted of a funnel hanging from the roof, with a small tray with straws to burn. If I did not read, I would whittle bits of wood I found in the forest, as the peasants were always doing. I admired their skill in carving small animals and figures. I decided to make a mezuzah case to be mounted on the doorpost. It was a complicated design, and when it was put up, Jews and Russians alike never failed to stop and look at it.

My employer had a store with supplies. The peasants would appear, as if out of nowhere. One or two of them in long coats and bark shoes were always waiting patiently on the porch. They brought fur pelts, a calf, or a few sheep instead of money. My employer bargained with them. In the end he had to record whether the peasant had credit left over or was owing him something. He took a stick and cut some marks, or made chalk marks on the window. He could not read or write, or even hold a pencil the right way. I told him that if he wanted, I would write things down in an account book. He was grateful for this. I relieved him of what was the most difficult part of his business for him.

It was unusual if we had a visitor. Months went by and maybe one peddler stopped. Once a Jew with a long beard down to his waist slept overnight. The next day, when he was about to leave, he said to Yeshovua, "I would like this tutor you've hired for my daughter Chaya," but that was all I heard about it.

A beggar passed through. Until a half year before, he had owned a factory in Moscow and been a prosperous man. Then the government had expelled all the Jews from that city on the first day of Passover—they didn't care for the plight of the thousands of Russian workers who lost their employment when the Jews left the city. I was not a revolutionary, but when I heard such stories I began to finally see that conditions were bad for everyone in Russia.

There certainly was no love for the regime among the peasants in this area. A few years before, a peasant claimed that she had a miraculous ikon, that those who touched it would be healed. People came to see it and left money and other offerings. Word of this traveled quickly, even to the ear of the governor of the province. No doubt so that he could supervise the collection boxes, he sent soldiers to the village to fetch the ikon. When the peasants refused to give it up, the soldiers cut branches in the forest and beat all the inhabitants, even women and children. In the end the ikon was seized and the most prominent village leaders were taken to jail. What was left behind was a seething bitterness. The peasants would show me the marks on their bodies left by the beatings.

My solitude led me to discouraged thoughts about the future. Even my taste for returning to Bessarabia left me.

My father came one day. To my inquiries about my mother, he answered that she was well, but I felt uneasy. Why did he act so nervous? "There's no reason for you to stop working," he told me. Why wouldn't he look me in the eyes? We talked only a short time, and then he went in to my employer.

I expected to see more of him, but he disappeared without even saying good-bye.

Yeshovua came over and said, "Your father came to collect your salary; he is coming back again at the end of next term."

I never saw a single kopeck of what I earned.

I was always restless. A premonition that there was something wrong at home never left me, and so I asked for permission to go for a visit. If my employer had not given it, I would have simply left. The nearer I came to Shumsk, the more worried I felt, and when I entered my home I felt a blackness descending over me. My grandmother, all bundled up in sweaters, was next to the stove and was crying. I caught sight of my brother with dirt on his face sitting on the floor. I ran into the next room, into darkness. Women floated about like ghosts, whispering and crying. My mother lay in a bed and looked small, light, her hands on the cover like claws, her yellow-looking face turned toward the wall. I leaned over the bed.

"Mother," I said. Her eyelids fluttered and she turned; she was breathing with difficulty, with a rasping breath.

Hindah said, "She's worried that they are going to draft you. Her only thoughts are of you."

I took my mother's hand, stroked her cheeks, and tried to calm her. Gradually she relaxed and fell into a heavy sleep. I stayed by her, crying quietly, a sense of terrible loss and regret growing in me. My sister wanted me to eat, but I was not hungry. Later my father came back from his prayers and we sat together in silence. The whole night passed and my mother woke several times but in a delirium from which she recognized no one.

My father and I went to the Bes Medresh for the morning services. I wanted to console him, but did not know how. It was a cold day and the snow on the ground was black. At the Bes Medresh there were a few clusters of people outside. My father and I pushed through without a word, but at the door Beryl the *shammes* stopped us. "No one can enter. A poor man slept inside last night and he died in his sleep. The corpse is still there. There will be no services." We turned around and walked slowly home.

When we had left, there had only been my family and a few neighbor women, but now the house was crowded. People kept arriving. When I saw this throng I had the pain of knowing the final moment was near. Somehow the news seeps out; everyone feels it.

Those who had wronged my mother came to ask forgiveness and say farewell. Others came to bear her company. My eyes were swimming with tears and all the faces blurred. For a few moments my mother regained consciousness. Standing beside her was my Aunt Deenah, who had traveled here even though she was in the final weeks of her pregnancy. My mother called her to her, and reached out to touch the new life stirring in Deenah's womb. The last words she uttered were to my aunt: "Have a girl, and name it after me."

All prayed as my mother's pure soul left her and ascended to a better world.

Then the rabbi's wife and the women of the town took charge. As they washed and shrouded the body, their loud weeping could be heard from our house. When they were finished, the men were allowed to return and wait with the body. We waited several hours, as the *rav* had decreed that the pauper must be buried first. Later the body was carried to the cemetery and the entire town of Shumsk came, and we mourned together in the deepest sorrow.

The death occurred on the seventh day of Adar,* and on the same day as Moses died. It was a holy day to all Jews, and now, consecrated by my mother's death, it had become holier yet to me.

At this time I might have returned to Bessarabia, but I decided I wanted to be near my family and help. I was certain this was what my mother would have wanted, and dead, she guided me more than she had when she was alive. I held myself responsible for her decline—why hadn't I written while I was at the tobacco plantation? My conscience was a raw wound. What had hurt her most was that I had let strangers become like mother and father to me. One day I wrote to Neci and Yankel to explain my situation and said again that it was unlikely they would see me again. This must have discouraged them because I received no further letters. And

* The sixth month of the Jewish year, usually falling in March.

it was better that way. I had no temptations, not for the easy life, not for the Arabian, and not for their love.

I returned to Zakit so that my salary would continue, but Yeshovua was generous about giving me days off so I could visit Shumsk. Whenever I came home, I saw how miserable the family was without my mother. Even when she was sick, she had held everything together. My father's character was not as strong as hers.

My grandmother grieved all the time that her child had died. My mother was more than a daughter-in-law to her. Each time I came, Grandmother was feebler and Hindah had more of a burden in caring for her.

Ten months passed in which I worked as a tutor and traveled home frequently. By watching over my younger brothers and sister I tried to atone for the way I had neglected my mother while she was alive. Then, as my mother had foreseen, my induction notice came. Immediately I quit my job and went to Shumsk so I could be with my family for the few days I had left before my service began.

On the Sunday after I arrived, my grandmother died in her sleep. I felt as if I had lost another mother.

～7

The military and the
matchmaker try to draft me

YAMPOLA, KREMENETS, AND KOSITONE, 1893

I HAD TO GO to the draft on Tuesday in Yampola. My father could
not accompany me because he had to stay home and sit *shivah.**

It was twenty versts to the induction center. Not a kopeck could
be spared, so I had to walk. I said good-bye, and even though I was
not a soldier yet, I began my first march. The weather was not particularly pleasant—and who knows what unexpected adventures a
Jew on foot might find? I kept thinking how it was better to be safe
inside a coach, or better yet to stay home.

After I had gone five versts I sat down for a rest. Suddenly,
without warning, a pack of about thirty dogs appeared; these animals, which were wild like wolves, frequently disturbed travelers.
I ran away with these creatures snapping at my heels. I do not
know how I was able to run so quickly. I came to a lime pit and
jumped in. At the bottom I found a big stick. Now I had my first
experience of military maneuvers. The dogs barked fiercely, and
whenever one got ready to spring at me, I whacked it with the
stick. I kept whirling here and there, until somehow a truce came
about between me and the pack. I stayed at the bottom of the pit,

---

* A week-long period of mourning.

and the dogs settled in a tight circle about the top, to rest and watch over me. I saw I had sentinels with vicious eyes, sharp teeth, and saliva dripping down their jaws. Every movement I made, they would snarl. I tried to be as still as possible and began to pray. It seemed like I would never escape, and in the end the dogs would conquer and be victorious.

The afternoon passed in this way, and I saw it was getting dark. Suddenly a coach came driving by and the noise disturbed the dogs so that they jumped to their feet and started barking again. The coach might have driven on, had the landowner inside not grown curious. He had his servant stop, and got out to inspect the scene. The two of them were able to chase the dogs away, and when they saw my predicament, the servant went to get a long rope. It was thrown down to me and I tied my hands to it and was pulled out. Immediately I began to thank my rescuer. We talked for a while and when he heard I was going to Yampola, he offered to give me a ride as far as Dederkale, which was on the way.

During the ride the landowner explained to me why he had been interested in the barking dogs. It seems recently an incident had occurred that involved the very pit where I had been trapped. A thief had stolen some horses from the landowner, under cover of darkness. When daylight came, the thief was afraid he would be caught. He led the horses to the pit, tied ropes about their necks, and then forced them in, strangling them in the process. Then he skinned them and left the carcasses. Soon the wild dogs gathered and began to fight with each other over who would have the largest share of the meat. Their barking aroused the attention of some peasants, who informed the landowner. At a nearby fair, they discovered the still-warm hides and were able to capture the thief.

This story was not particularly soothing to me after my recent experience, but I was nonetheless grateful to be in a coach, safe from attackers. The ride went along without event. The only time we stopped was when my companion noticed one of those grottoes by the side of the road with an ikon. Being a religious man, he stopped the coach and got out to cross himself in front of the shrine of Saint Nicholas. It was late at night when we came to Dederkale. The landowner let me off in front of an inn.

I went inside and found the place filled with Russians who, like myself, were going to the draft board the next day to serve in the czar's army. They drank and sang boisterously as if it were a celebration. Someone arrived with an accordion. Because I had no money, I sat by myself and observed what was happening around me. Fortunately no one seemed to care about my presence; no one hindered or helped me. I was able to stay all night and have a roof over my head and a chair for my bed, instead of the cold earth. The next day, too, I had good luck. A peasant gave me a ride in his wagon directly to the draft induction center.

I was immediately given a number and asked to wait. I noticed a tall soldier with a red face calling the numbers by lottery. All of Wednesday I sat and waited, but mine was not called. The next day I returned and was not bored or impatient. I got to observe the Russian army's induction process. When a goy passed his medical, he was generally permitted to go home for a month before reporting. A Jew who passed his physical emerged from the examination room under guard, and was taken immediately to the barracks.

Among Jewish sons, each had brought a mother who cried and shivered and when he went off to the barracks began to mourn right there at the induction center, as if her child had been sent to the other world. Extraordinary efforts were made to avoid the draft even at the last moment. In the morning a young man was sound, but after lunch his condition had changed. One pulled out all his teeth, another blinded himself in one eye. Others relied solely on money, but this was not safe, as the officials would take the bribe and then inform on them.

Beside me was a youth with long *peyes*. His face was so emaciated that it resembled a dry fig. And next to him was not one, but two mothers—his own and his wife's. I heard that his father-in-law was a rich man. I thought, "*Nah*, it is certain in this case—given the money, the parents, the condition he is in from fasting—that God is going to help." The soldier who called the numbers announced my companion's and mine too. Naturally I stood up. When the young man beside me rose, it was with a mother on each side. He dragged along and could barely move. Everyone envied his decrepitude. In contrast, I walked unassisted. I overheard someone comment about me, "He's a healthy, well-built young man with strong muscles. Poor thing, he's finished."

We entered the examination room where a military council sat around a table. There was a Gorodskoi doctor and one from Vienna with a wrinkled face, white hair, and a monocle. The young man was to be first. I saw a bundle of bones which were barely holding together, stumbling forward in a weaving, drunken motion. He managed to make it to the scale and was weighed. The Gorodskoi doctor asked him, "What is your problem? Why are you so emaciated?"

He answered in a quavering voice, "I don't know."

One of the members of the military council called out, "Are you married?"

"Yes."

"Do you have children?"

"Yes, two," said the young man and seemed about to faint from the exertion.

His interrogator announced, "If such a soul can have children, he can also be a soldier. The soldier's bread will revive him." The doctor signed his signature to the induction forms while a soldier assisted the young man to get dressed, as he was not capable of doing it himself.

Meanwhile the word spread to those who were assembled outside that a Jewish son had been inducted. Moaning and crying began. I was embarrassed for the young man. I was humiliated for my people. It pained me that Jews acted with so little dignity. When a goy went in to be examined, no one knew whether or not he was drafted. No screaming was ever heard to call attention to the fact. There was just quiet. But when a Jew was called, the situation was different. First of all, only one Jew in ten had not maimed himself, and among those who were drafted, armed soldiers had to guard them to see that there were no escapes.

The effect of all this on me was that I became determined that I would set a better example. I began to think I might enjoy being a soldier, and the idea appealed to me more and more. I imagined myself in a gorgeous uniform like the officers at the port near Cotu

Mori. I was sure I would have the opportunity to demonstrate how well I could ride and be promoted into the cavalry, and there I would receive an excellent horse. In battle, I saw myself bravely leading the attack, jumping over the barricades and into the enemy lines. As I was waiting my turn to be examined, I began to quietly hum the Russian national anthem.

My name was called. I hurried eagerly to the scale, and the Vienna doctor called out loud that I had passed the height and weight test. He asked me, "Are you healthy?"

I answered, "I am not deficient in anything. I am courageous to the seventh heaven and I am ready to serve the czar father. I wish to be drafted at once."

The doctor looked at me in a perplexed way. "Have you been ill recently? Have you suffered from brain fever?"

"No," I objected vehemently, but already the doctor had called out "blue ticket" and was signaling he was ready for the next inductee. It was no good to object. My hopes were shattered.

I came out and Jews gathered about me and congratulated me that I had received an exemption. I felt downcast. That day I left for home with the realization that I must accept my fate; I would never be a soldier. My only battle was to be the one I had had with the pack of dogs.

I happened to arrive home when my father was entertaining a guest. Whether Yisroel Yehosayit the matchmaker had been invited, I cannot say. He came without invitations. He sat at the table with a cup of tea in one hand and, in the other, his little book in which he took a census of the unmarried children in a family and their ages. Also he concerned himself with widowers like my father. Just as I came through the door he was suggesting for my father a woman named Devorah who would bring a small dowry.

My arrival astonished everyone. My six-year-old brother Yossel cried, "Where is your uniform?" The guest and the rest of my family gathered around me, and I had to explain all the details of how I had managed to come back. When I was finished, my father said we should celebrate and Hindah searched for some brandy. It turns out there were a few drops and I, my brother Beryl, my father, and Yisroel Yehosayit wet our throats with some. Yisroel was enthusiastic about my exemption, and before he left he insisted on interviewing me and writing a description of me in his book.

In the next few months he went about from place to place saying that in Shumsk a young man was available who was healthy, handsome, fluent in Russian, and, best of all, in possession of a blue ticket. His efforts soon brought results. I had an appointment to go to Kremenets to meet a girl named Miriam Shtrak, the daughter of a wealthy businessman.

I dressed myself in the best clothes I had and took a coach to that city. There I inquired where I could find Aaron Shtrak and was directed to a shop. The father was away, having driven to Orinka to General Babrikov for an order, but the mother and daughter welcomed me graciously. We drank tea drawn from an enormous brass samovar and I was shown every attention. I was grateful to be received as a suitor. I knew there was a big difference between our positions in life. I was the son of a pauper, and here were people who owned a prosperous business, a store which I saw was piled high with bolts of cloth, pots, pans, soap, and all manner of goods.

Miriam seemed pleasant. I did not really get a good look at her. She was constantly getting up to attend to something, acting rather nervous. If I glanced at her, her face would flush and she would look away. Anyway, her mother, an elderly woman in a black silk dress, kept me busy with her talking.

Soon our conversation was interrupted. The bell above the shop began ringing and my hostesses had to excuse themselves. Customers could not be kept waiting. The store crowded with people and I was invited to help. I guessed the mother wanted to observe me, and I took special care that my behavior was perfect.

I was efficient and polite as I waited on one customer after another. If it was a Jew I spoke Yiddish and wrote the order in Yiddish, and if it was a Russian I spoke fluently in his tongue and perhaps he felt comfortable with me and took home a little more than he first intended. The mother passed by and told me she was impressed that I could write orders in Russian. I was kept so busy that only occasionally did I catch a glimpse of Miriam. All I saw was her running about to fill orders.

Then, around five o'clock, suddenly it was silent. At first I could not understand what had happened. Everyone stood around as if a great dignitary had arrived. I looked here and there and finally I noticed a Jew had walked in with a stiff posture who had a harelip. Perhaps it was because of the deformity, but his face had an unpleasant expression, and everything he looked at seemed to displease him. I wondered who this person could be. Miriam went up to him and began whispering in his ear. Not once did he turn to her. When she finished he looked me over. "So you're the one," he said. I would have thought up an answer, but he turned on his heel and went across to a hall that led to the living quarters. I comprehended that I had just met the father, Harav Aaron Shtrak.

Miriam said, "My father is a little tired. After dinner he will feel better. You will stay and eat with us."

I have never witnessed such a dinner as I did that night. It seems Harav Shtrak was an autocrat; he gave commands and had to be obeyed. Everyone trembled. Because of his harelip he could not hold anything in his mouth, but he chose to blame it on how his food was prepared. Each dish that was brought to him was cause for a new outbreak of temper. It had to be returned to the kitchen and something else brought immediately. Neither his wife nor his daughter was permitted to sit down for a second. They ran back and forth, with him shouting after them. I wondered when the meal would be over. When his wife was in tears, Harav Shtrak was finally satisfied.

He announced that no more food was to be brought; it was time to interrogate the suitor. "What work have you done?" he demanded.

I answered simply, "I've been a tutor."

A look of contempt passed over his features. Perhaps he did not think it was proper to give a three-thousand-ruble dowry to a lowly tutor. Even so, he continued to question me in his abrupt way. I felt disgusted. Finally I said, "Why do you have to question me like this? If you like me, retain me. If not, I have no complaints against anyone. I will go home."

A despot does not take such an answer with grace. His face turned red. He jumped up from the table and shouted, "You . . . get out of my house!" Then he marched out of the room.

I got up slowly and intended to go. Suddenly Miriam gave a cry. Her mother tried to hold her, but she threw herself in my path. She grabbed my hand and said, "Please . . . I'm begging you, don't . . . just wait . . . a little longer. . . ." Her manner was desperate. I felt so sorry for her that I said I would stay.

She ran after her father. The mother and I stood motionless and listened to their voices through the wall. As Miriam pleaded with her father, he became more enraged. I could imagine from what I heard that she was crawling on her knees after him and kissing his boots, but this did not appease him. He started to curse his daughter and ordered her out.

In a moment she burst into the room with a wild look, rushed to her mother, began embracing her, and said, "Dear mother, I beg you to talk to him for me." A lamp was shining full on Miriam's face and she had a peaked, unhealthy look. I noticed for the first time that she and her mother both seemed aged beyond their years. The mother said in a weary, toneless voice, "I have no business with your crazy father. Leave him alone." Miriam collapsed on the floor and began to weep without restraint.

I felt that my presence only made the situation worse and resolved to leave. I got up and went to the hallway which led outside, and the mother followed after me and indicated she had something to tell me. We stopped in the doorway and for a long time she struggled to find the right words. In the end all she said was, "My daughter is twelve years older than you. The difference in your ages makes the match inappropriate."

I traveled home to Shumsk. I rested. The next morning I went to the Bes Medresh and afterward worked in our garden. Right before lunch the matchmaker arrived. My father's suit to Devorah was being carried forward and he had a few details to arrange. I was disgusted with the whole business. When I told Yisroel what

happened in Kremenets, he only shrugged and was not discouraged or even embarrassed he had deceived me by neglecting
to mention Miriam's age. He murmured something about how
Aaron Shtrak ruined all of his daughter's chances. So he had
known all along the outcome of my visit. He was a wheedling,
persuasive man and soothed me with flattering words and
promises.

When I was calmer, he told me about another match, a girl
named Esther who lived in Kositone. She was rich, beautiful, intelligent, well educated, and only eighteen years of age. After I
had agreed to go to meet her, he confessed that she had one minor
defect and that was an almost imperceptible limp. I agreed with
him that such a problem was "hardly worth mention." I begged
my sister to press my suit and she did this so skillfully that none of
the wrinkles of my trip to Kremenets showed when I dressed myself up and began my second journey.

I arrived in Kositone in the afternoon and was met by a servant
who took me to a large house. Inside he led me through a series of
rooms and I saw from the furnishings that this was a much wealthi-
er family than Miriam's. In a sitting room my host and hostess, the
girl's aunt and uncle, awaited me. Both of them looked somewhat
similar: short, plump, and rosy-cheeked. The aunt had a girlish
voice and laughed a lot when we were introduced. I never met
people of such excellent manners. They put me at ease at once.
The aunt spoke kindly. She had the servant bring in delicious
food—small, delicate cakes that melted in the mouth as if they
were made of air. She wanted to know if I needed another pillow
or if I wanted another cup of tea.

The uncle spoke in a soft, refined voice. "I better tell you a little
about Esther's history. When Esther was six she was run over by a
coach. The best specialists were summoned and worked with all
their skill and saved her life—but did not prevent her from becoming a cripple. Soon after the accident, both of Esther's parents
died from typhus. Her grandfather loved her dearly and took her
to live with him and gave her an excellent upbringing. When he

died, he left her as his sole heir and appointed my wife and me as her guardians until she married."

I asked, "Why is it that you are considering a poor boy for the groom of an heiress?"

"The matchmaker praised you highly as an exceptional person," the aunt said, and I accepted this answer.

When I looked over at her, she had her handkerchief to her eyes and appeared to be crying.

"Poor dear, so many years ago it happened, but every time my wife is reminded of Esther's accident she cries her heart out for her."

"No more than you do, my husband."

"Such love for a niece is unusual," I said.

"Oh, but to us she is our child."

"Our only child," he echoed.

"But we are concerned for you, David. You must consider well before you marry a wife with such a . . ." She let out a soft sigh.

"Yes, we want Esther to have a husband, but think well before you rush into anything."

This certainly was different from the reception I had received from Aaron Shtrak, and I felt I was dealing with people with extremely sensitive feelings. Even though they hinted she might have a more severe defect than I had been led to believe, I was not discouraged. Instead I felt eager to meet the child who had inspired such love in her relatives. But the girl remained absent throughout the interview.

Finally I asked if I might see her.

The uncle said, "Come," and led me over to a door with panes of glass. "Look, she sits out there."

I saw a garden thick with fruit trees just beginning to put out a few green leaves, and with a stone bench in one corner. On it sat a delicate-looking girl reading a book and unaware of her uncle and me observing her. I had never seen the color of her hair among Jewish daughters, only sometimes in peasant children. It was a white-gold. Her eyes were large and the palest shade of blue, her skin like milk. Her features were lovely to me, glowing and spiritual, and there was a serenity in the repose of her body. It seemed to me I was seeing an angel, not someone of this world. I remembered Sasa, and how I had admired her looks. Next to Esther, Sasa was crude and clumsy.

I stood gazing awhile, then said to the uncle, "May I go out to her?"

He took my arm. "Come back and sit on the couch." When I was seated again, he explained, "I want to spare my niece any unnecessary upset. First you must come to Kositone so I can observe your character. You will work at a store which my cousin owns. If I see you are an upstanding person, as I am sure you will prove yourself to be, then you can meet Esther."

Esther inspired tender feelings in me, and I did not want to be less solicitous than her uncle, so I agreed at once. I even mentioned how touching I found his devotion to his niece.

This pleased the uncle and he said, "Between people who revere piety, no papers need to be drawn up."

When his wife asked if I objected to this, her husband immediately silenced her, saying, "Be careful. He doesn't deserve to have his feelings hurt like this."

What was I to say? I consented to having no betrothal contract written as well.

In a short while I was settled with the family of the cousin and working as a shopkeeper. Proskurov was nearby and when my Aunt Bobbah and Uncle Nuchem heard I was there, my aunt came herself and begged me to visit. They gave me a more pleasant reception than I had received before and seemed anxious to make up for their past behavior. My aunt began to think about the situation and how close I was to Proskurov, and suddenly it occurred to her that I could come live with her and stay in my old room, the *sukkah*. Once this idea took hold of her mind, she began to insist upon it.

It was a mystery to me that someone could change like this, but that is what happened. As much as she wanted to get rid of me before, now that I did not need her assistance she was clutching me to her. She even rebuked my uncle—why hadn't he seen that some cloth from the store was put aside and made into a suit for me? It was with the greatest difficulty that I extricated myself that evening and went back to the cousin's store, and I know when I left that Aunt Bobbah was offended.

No one knew better than I how hard it was to appease her. It happened that within the month I came upon the means to make everything all right between us. I had written to several people in Kishinev, including the *rav* who had assisted me with my problems with Mendel. From him Neci and Yankel had gotten my new address. I thought they had forgotten me, but it was not true. They were large-hearted people, and I received the first of many gifts that came to me from them. It was a huge crate containing items that were the greatest luxuries outside of Bessarabia: a barrel of wine, a ten-pound bag of nuts, a sack of sugar, and a box of oranges and one of lemons. I took everything to Aunt Bobbah and told her I would share future gifts with her, and she was reconciled to me.

After this she never ceased to talk about the present I had given her and how it showed what a devoted and loving nephew I was. My affection was proof to the world of how well she had treated me. Why would I give her presents if I didn't feel obligated? Now whenever my name was mentioned, Aunt Bobbah was my supporter and advocate. All my good traits were a reflection of her excellent training. When we met a stranger, she said, "This is my son David." Later she took them aside to explain what she meant by "son," as if to mention in my presence that I was only a nephew would be too detrimental to my feelings.

I accepted all this. There was no harm in it, and I was glad we were on good terms.

I worked. I began to accumulate some savings from my wages, and several months passed. I kept thinking about Esther and tried to visit her, but somehow I was always turned away with an excuse. When Aunt Bobbah heard about this she said that I was being insulted, she was being insulted—in fact, our whole family was being insulted—and I should leave Kositone at once. My arguments that Esther's guardians were people of moral rectitude made no impression on her. She had bitter words for them, and Esther as well. When my aunt said, "Would you marry a cripple if she wasn't rich?" I answered, "What if she became crippled after I married her? Would I then abandon my wife?" She had another argument for me. She said the girl must be severely deformed and that was why they hid her away.

I could not believe her and would not let myself be persuaded by her suspicions. I was confident and trusting that when Passover came I would be invited to the first seder at my future bride's. As it turned out, I did not even receive an invitation to the second. At Purim, too, I had not received the traditional present of pastries that are sent out even to casual acquaintances. How could a groom be overlooked? Perhaps there was some truth in what Aunt Bobbah said. I went to Esther's guardians and insisted on visiting with the girl. This concession was made. I was to be permitted to take her on a walk to the boulevard.

I came to fetch her one afternoon. At closer sight she was far more beautiful than I had realized in that brief glimpse from her uncle's sitting room window. She greeted me and her speech was gentle and to my ears seemed even noble. When she put her arm in mine and we moved along the street, my heart twisted with pain for her. It was not simply a "limp." I saw she could barely walk. There had been some truth in what Aunt Bobbah suggested about Esther's condition—a perfect creature had been marred by an accident. All I could think of was that I must find a place for us to sit down as soon as possible.

Fortunately we came to a bench. I felt more composed once she was removed from that agony of walking. It was a mild day; the trees along the boulevard were in bud and the birds were singing. Occasionally a flock of them would rise in the air and then settle on the branches again. Carriages rolled over the cobblestones; people strolled along in lovely clothes. We said little. Conversation between us was difficult. If our eyes happened to meet, she smiled at me so sweetly that I felt an urge to press her hands between mine, to feel the warmth of her skin. I wanted to tell her that her infirmity would never hinder my affection. I considered her higher than myself. I was startled when I saw tears in her eyes.

"What's the matter? What's wrong?" I asked.

"It is bitter when one must do what others demand and cannot do what one's own conscience dictates." She began to weep. I urged her to unburden her heart. She struggled to control herself and then said, "I realize how disappointed my aunt and uncle were when my grandfather overlooked them and left everything to me. They feel I have robbed them. I know that they will not permit me to marry because they will never give up control of my inheritance. I have reconciled myself to this. It torments me that you have been deceived. They pretend I am affianced to you to keep up appearances before the world, and they thought that a poor boy would be less likely to complain than one from a rich family."

When I heard this I was furious. I threatened to expose the aunt and uncle, but Esther pleaded with me that I must not. She said, "All I ask is that you go home, because you have no hope here." I saw she was in earnest and so I said, "Let's not talk of this any longer." I called a droshky and took her back.

Later I went to my employer, collected my wages, and told him I received word my father was getting married and I wanted to go home for a visit.

When I came home, the marriage was already accomplished. My poor father had married a shrew. She threw dishes at him. Devorah was cruel. She decided that she did not want "another woman's children" and broke up the family. Hindah was sent to live with her in-laws. My sister Shivah became a maid in Viliya. My brother Beryl was a teacher in a village, and my two small brothers, one ten and the other seven, remained and were tormented by their stepmother. My father crept meekly about and dared not interfere. I saw my mother's grieving spirit in every corner of the house. How much love she had lavished on her children, and look what it had come to.

I felt heartbroken. There was no home for me here. Once again I debated with myself whether I should go back to Bessarabia, but the guilt over my mother's death kept me chained to the place. For the sake of my two youngest brothers, I had to try to stay nearby. Now more than ever they needed me.

* * *

I sought out Yisroel, and he had a new match ready for me. The girl lived in Tureni, a few versts from Shumsk. Since it was close, my father and stepmother decided to accompany me. We drove there in a wagon and arrived in the early evening just after the cows had been milked. The household consisted of Moishe and Malke and their daughter Chaya, a young girl, rather nice-looking but exceptionally shy. She kept by her mother and would not even look at me. The father seemed familiar, but I could not remember where we had met. He offered to take care of the horses while we went inside, but since he was an old man I insisted on doing the necessary chores myself.

When I went inside, everyone was gathered about the table and waiting for me before dinner was begun. I washed and prayed and took my place on a sturdy wooden chair that was left for me. A simple meal of noodles and cheese was served. We were all given ample portions and began to eat. I felt comfortable here and thought I was glad I had not fallen into the riches in Kremenets or Kositone. Didn't the Torah tell us that it was forbidden for animals of different species like an ox and a horse to be yoked together? And so neither should rich and poor be yoked together.

I kept glancing at Moishe and trying to remember where I had met him. Then it came to me. He was the old man who had visited Yeshovua Greenshpan one night. Shortly after this insight, he affirmed my memory. The moment the meal was finished he addressed me in the following manner:

"The first time I met you was when I was passing through Zakit. I went straight home and told everyone I saw in Zakit a young man with a torn cap and ragged clothes who was teaching children and I would like to have him for my Chaya. Now, since you are still a bachelor, it appears my words are being fulfilled. I know you are poor and have nothing. Here you have a garden, four cows, a horse, a wagon, dogs, a silo with groats, a shop, and also a few spare rubles. We are already an old couple and I have little strength left. Here, take everything I possess, and my wife and I will live with you. What do you think? This very day invitations will be sent to Viliya and the articles of engagement will be written."

I was so astonished by Moishe's haste that I did not know what to say. Just as Esther's guardians had delayed, this father was in a rush. My stepmother pulled on my sleeve and dragged my father and me over to a corner of the room where she exploded with a loud whisper, "Something is wrong. Why is he trying to push you into this?"

The moment I saw she was against the match, I suddenly felt I was for it. I answered, "I have wasted a year in Kositone and now I will make it up. They want to rush only because they are old and alone in the world."

Moishe, of course, guessed what we were discussing and he called out, "I tell you the truth: I like David. So does my wife and my child. So why in this life should we delay?"

I replied, "Let it be."

A letter was sent to Viliya at once so that the articles of engagement could be drawn and I was determined to go wherever my fate took me. Later that night several people arrived and the articles of engagement were written. In fact, I wrote them myself. My father-in-law took out a thick book and turned the pages, and hundreds of rumpled ruble notes fell out. "Here," he said, "is the dowry, and next Sunday I am coming directly to Shumsk and will place the dowry with a trustee."

When I left I realized the entire time I had not said a single word to the bride. As we rode back to Shumsk my father sat with a morose expression and my stepmother passed the time with such remarks as "You know what you have done? You have butchered yourself with a dull blade."

In the following days she sat in triumph as the busybodies of the town came to congratulate me. Foremost among these was Shifra, my father's new sister-in-law. Aunt Shifra said, "If your mother rose from the grave and witnessed what you are doing, she would drop dead once again. Why are you lying down on a sickbed?"

"Is the bride sick?" I asked.

Aunt Shifra replied, "Well, your in-laws once had a son Pini. Tuesday he married. Wednesday his parents returned home. Thursday a messenger came to say he was sick . . . and Friday he died."

By the time she had completed this little calendar, more of Devorah's friends and relations had squeezed into the house to get a glimpse of me. One frightened me with a mournful cry followed by a litany that echoed from several throats: "A golden child has met his doom."

A woman was pushed forward by the others and she told this story: "There was also a daughter Pesi that belonged to your in-laws. She was engaged to the Ayupler *hazzan*'s boy, Gerson. Three-quarters of a year after the wedding, Gerson died and left her with child."

I asked, "Do you have anything more to inform me about?"

Aunt Shifra gave a shriek. "Is this not enough?"

I addressed the women: "Well, you've taken great trouble to give me these histories, but it was unnecessary. What you tell could have happened to anyone. People get sick and die. One does not pick the day. Is Pesi to blame that her husband died? No wonder with such evil, idle gossip that my in-laws wish to get the wedding over with quickly."

"Well," Devorah said, "what about the crippled girl? You have abandoned her."

This infuriated me. I screamed in a loud voice to be certain all of these women heard, "Am I to blame when I waited a year in Kositone and nothing happened? I am no prophet and I did not know what goes on in people's hearts. All I saw was that they ignored me and did nothing."

This speech was interrupted because at this point a telegram arrived from Proskurov from Aunt Bobbah and Uncle Nuchem which said: "Why have you committed yourself to this engagement without consulting us? You never should have done it. We were going to set you up in the lumber business and you would have made over ten thousand rubles. Then we were going to marry you off and you would have lived like a god in Odessa." I saw suddenly, when I was no longer free, the world was full of opportunities that I had missed.

I wanted to escape the house, even for a moment. I told my stepmother I would get her some fresh water from the well and went outside to the backyard. I lowered the pail, filled it, and tried to pull it up. It had caught on something and I leaned well over the edge and began to tug on the rope with all my might. Unfortunately the rope was frayed and snapped and the pail dropped into the water. I fell over head first and down some twenty-five feet. The water reached over my head and I was choking. When I came to the surface I screamed for help. People heard my shouts and came. They let down a rope and pulled me out. All this took a long time.

I was unconscious later, just as when I had hurt my head in Bessarabia. When I opened my eyes I was surrounded by a doctor and several neighbors, along with my family. The first words that were said to me were, "You see how quickly the Almighty punishes you for abandoning a cripple?" I was too sick to answer. It almost killed me, this marriage business.

After two weeks I recovered. I learned the dowry had been placed precisely when my father-in-law had promised and the date of the wedding was set. The town of Shumsk rang like a bell: "David is a groom."

~8

I take a wife but feel depressed

THE WEDDING WAS the first Wednesday in September. My bride and I were both in our eighteenth year of life. I awoke that morning, said my prayers for my sins so that I might enter the marriage a pure person, and fasted. Soon everyone in our household was rushing about getting dressed. At the same time friends and relations in their best finery arrived to await the coaches my father had hired. I was glad when they came and our journey to Tureni could begin. Although there were six coaches, they were not spacious enough and everyone had to squeeze together. Even so, along the way we collected more guests. At Zakit we stopped at the home of my former employer, Yeshovua Greenshpan. He had hired a coach too and loaded it with a barrel of brandy. This thoughtfulness was appreciated. It was an unusually hot day for this time of year and people could barely slake their thirst. Cups of brandy were passed from hand to hand, and occasionally we had to stop the coaches to make sure people had enough. Soon everyone was merry and singing, even my stepmother.

One coach followed another in a long snakelike line and we entered the path leading to Tureni. It was cool and dark. The deeper we went into the forest, the thicker the trees became, and the rougher the forest floor so that the coaches jolted us this way and that. But no one cared; it only added to the hilarity. People were making jokes because I was to be a bridegroom. I laughed along and joined the cheerful mood.

The afternoon went by. I saw it had become late, almost night, and the landscape was unfamiliar. The drivers stopped and consulted. Then a different one took the lead of the caravan of coaches. My father muttered, "We should have been there by now." This was the thought in everyone's mind and I began to see anxious expressions about me. It was colder. I looked out the window and saw that a great number of trees were dry or dead. For a moment it flashed through my mind how bleak and lonely it would be to live here in winter, and the thought was enough to make me shudder.

It became completely black. Not a ray of moonlight could penetrate the trees. The drivers refused to go on, and who could blame them? It was useless to wander about in the dark, and also it was dangerous for the horses because they might stumble and fall. There we all were, dressed in our best clothes and wondering what to do. We climbed down. We were all worried but tried to control ourselves. Some of the small children began to cry. Then one started screaming that he heard a bear growling. I do not think there was a bear near, but it was possible, as there were many living in the wilderness of the forest. Panic spread and people began to run blindly about, many falling over roots or bumping into trees.

I thought a tragedy would result. But I was mistaken. Suddenly something astonishing happened. The sounds of a trombone, a viol, and a drum began to drift through the forest. Immediately we began to shout to come save us. Flickering candles came nearer. They were carried by the wedding musicians. When we had not arrived, Moishe decided we must be lost and sent the musicians to search for us. They came up to us, gave us the candles, and then played a march and led us triumphantly to Tureni. There a large crowd greeted us with cheers.

Moishe came over to me. His manner was nervous, even a little cold, and I felt it must be because he had been upset when we did not come before. I said to him, "Don't worry, we can begin right

Malke and Moishe, David Toback's in-laws, and their two granddaughters (Russia, 1910). This photo was taken to soothe Chaya's homesickness. Note the straw on the ground and the painted backdrop.

away." He agreed that was what he wanted, and rushed off to consult with the rabbi, who was waiting. I noticed my relatives from Proskurov. I was delighted they had traveled so far for my sake, and before I did anything else I had to stop to talk with them. My aunt's first words were "I don't like the reception your in-laws are giving to our family." I tried to pacify her, but with Aunt Bobbah it was not easy.

We did not finish our conversation because Moishe had sent some young men to help me dress. They took me to a bedroom, and the contents of my pockets were emptied and a *kittel** put on me. Then I was taken to the bride. She sat there pale and tense-looking, all dressed in white. I saw her face only an instant. A veil was thrown over her head. I wanted to comfort her and tell her not to be afraid. Instead I had to give the customary discourse on her duties as a wife.

When this was done, I was taken outside. A beautiful scene greeted me. Each guest held a candle. Nearby was a *huppa†* of a richly embroidered cloth and beneath it stood a rabbi with a smiling face and a long, white beard. I went to stand before him. Everyone began to murmur, "They are leading the bride." Chaya appeared and slowly made her way toward me. In a deep, melodic voice the rabbi began to intone the benedictions, and my heart overflowed with tenderness for my young bride. Tonight I was alive in a way I had never been before. At last I would fulfill my manhood. A goblet was thrown on the floor. I stamped on it vigorously and it shattered. I gave a ring to Chaya and we were married.

Cries of *Mazel tov!* came from the crowd. I stepped from beneath the *huppa.* One moment Chaya was on my arm, and then suddenly she had disappeared. I struggled to follow after her, but my friends locked my arms in theirs, drowned my words with congratulations, and drew me forward to the wedding feast. Tables were covered with food. My in-laws had been excessive in their hospitality—not even this crowd could finish all that was laid out.

---

* A white ceremonial robe.
† The canopy under which the marriage ceremony is performed.

My companions released me and began to help themselves to the rich puddings, the platters of fish and chopped liver.

I looked for Chaya but could not find her in the crowd. Instead I discovered my Aunt Bobbah again. This time she was in a truly bad temper. She seized my arm and said, "I don't care if you just got married. Leave this place immediately."

"I don't understand."

"Take a look at your in-laws and your bride, and you will. They held themselves in a little before the service, but now they're humiliating us."

I told my aunt it was not possible for me to leave my wife, and she said, "I'm sorry. Good-bye, David."

She found my uncle and the two of them walked away with great dignity and soon left the wedding. They even took their wedding gift away with them. A few people had watched this scene, but when I looked at them inquiringly they averted their eyes.

I began to search for my in-laws and my wife. I found them sitting to one side. Their expressions were fit for a funeral. Moishe was grim. Malke's face was contorted, and Chaya's head was bowed. Several times I demanded what was the matter, but they would not answer. I left them to try to find someone who would. I saw my father drinking and with a smile on his lips. Apparently he had not discovered something was wrong, and I did not want to disturb him. I looked about for a wedding guest related to Moishe and Malke. Someone had instructed the musicians to play. The blare of the music grated on me. It was too loud, too much, just as there was too much food. All this excess was covering up some secret. For the first time I began to consider how hastily I had consented to the marriage. On what basis had I taken such an important step in my life? To spite my stepmother. To get the whole business finished and not be bothered anymore. Now I was being punished.

People avoided me. Only one couple did not notice my approach. These two were Asher and Genendel, and not only were they related to my in-laws, but I knew them well because they lived in Zakit. Asher, a man with a round face and plump hands, was bent over a platter of fish and picking out the best pieces. Several he rejected, but finally with a sigh, he settled upon one for his plate and another for his wife's. Genendel immediately busied herself with peeling the skins and removing the bones.

I went over to them and said, "My in-laws have shamed me."

Asher lifted his eyebrows and Genendel chewed vigorously on a morsel she had in her mouth. As soon as she was done with it she said to me, "What do you mean?" Before I could answer she turned to Asher and asked, "Do you think it's too salty?"

"Maybe . . . maybe . . . it's hard to tell with the first bite."

"Well, take another taste to see."

I asked, "Why do they seem so puffed up and angry?"

Again I had to wait until they were finished chewing. "No, Asher dear, it's not too salty." Asher took another forkful of fish and then as he held it in midair, close to its destination, he addressed me.

"The truth is, they had a tragedy."

"Yes, I know. Their son-in-law died."

"No, no. Not that tragedy. There is a more recent one."

"I think it's too peppery," Genendel said.

"More recent one?"

"Yes, this tragedy is only just beginning. They got caught selling brandy and your wife and in-laws are going to have to spend a few months in prison—maybe more. Who knows? They have to leave in two days, I believe. Please don't say anything. They'll be angry if we are the ones to have informed you."

"I won't."

"You promise?"

"Yes, I do."

Asher's face broke into a large smile. "You know what? The fish is truly good."

He bent over the platter again and did not notice my departure. To him the fish was more important than I was, since I had just married into a family that was going to jail.

Later that night my bride awaited me. I came into our bedroom where she held the covers tightly about her with a trembling hand. She looked at me with such intensity that all words dried on my lips, and I blew the lamp out so that I would not see her eyes boring into me. Then I lay down beside her, but I felt awkward and was afraid to touch her. A long time passed in which we just lay there quietly. Perhaps it was an hour, maybe more. I kept wanting to reach out to Chaya, but my hands were paralyzed. I believed she was staring into the darkness and thinking of me as I did of her. But I was mistaken. Her terror about going to jail drove all other thoughts from her mind.

Suddenly she startled me with a cry. From her lips came sobs. "I don't want to go away. . . . They'll hurt me in jail. . . . Save me. . . . save me! . . ." She said these words over and over, but after a while I hardly heard. There was a beating in my ears and I remembered the veil which had descended over her head. Now in the darkness it seemed as if it were covering Chaya once again, and me as well.

It was two days later that they went to prison. Almost the moment they left I was sick with loneliness. But it was necessary that I remain in Tureni to take care of my father-in-law's business and everything else. Each day was a struggle for me. I had to wake up early to tend the animals; then I divided my time between the store, the house, and working in the garden. Finally I decided to hire a Russian maid to help me. There was an extra room she could stay in and I didn't have to pay much.

I felt a little better now that I had someone around, but after a few days passed I saw there was going to be trouble. The girl was young and pretty, and the peasants would come and harass her. I handled the situation the best I could. I wanted to protect the girl, but at the same time I did not want to antagonize the peasants. They seemed rougher and more quick-tempered than others I had known. There were even rumors that crimes had been committed and gone unpunished. Tureni was remote and no one bothered with what happened here. Things were settled by the villagers in their own ways and no one could interfere. There was a church near here, but even the priest had little influence. No matter how much he protested, the peasants carried out their superstitious practices. When a sickness was going around, one night the young women went out half-naked and drew a plough around the village in order to exorcise the demons. I heard they carried whips in case anyone came out to look at them.

The priest did not live far from me. He was a poor man who had to work his own garden in order to have enough to eat. The only way he could be distinguished from the other peasants was by a special high hat he wore. The others distrusted him because they were poor, but they still had to contribute something to his salary and for the upkeep of the church. The church was a tall, narrow building that looked like a granary. From the outside, at least, it looked very crude. Whatever the peasants gave the priest, it wasn't much. So there was little to envy the priest about—even his family life was a misfortune. The bishop had forced him to marry the daughter of the old priest to provide a home for his mother-in-law and all the children. His wife turned out to be a shrew, and everyone tried to avoid her.

Of all the peasants, the one who frightened me the most was the one named Mechalke. To me he looked exactly like a ferocious beast with flat face and a hairy body like a bear's. Like the others he parted his hair in the middle and shaved it off in a straight line in the back of his neck. He wore dark trousers, a dirty red shirt fastened at the side of his neck, with a thick belt around his waist. On his feet he wore coarse thick socks with strips of cloth wound round his legs and attached to bast shoes. He had a fist that could give a substantial blow, and a bad disposition to match. One day he informed me he wanted me to sell brandy. I said, "Look, my family is in jail for doing that."

He answered, "You better not give excuses. With me looking after you, no one is going to inform on you and no one is going to harm you."

What choice did I have? I went to a place where I knew I could get a few barrels of brandy, and Moishe's house was turned into a tavern.

The devil brought Mechalke to me every night. Mechalke was my foremost customer. I would pour him drinks and listen to his secrets. It seems that a Jew was better even than a priest for confession. I was the outsider and it was my fate to witness events and receive unwanted confidences. If a word of what Mechalke told me had leaked out, I would have been killed—but first, so I would not get off too easily, I would have been tortured. The reason for this was that Mechalke was committing the worst crime known to these peasants. He was stealing horses, and their livestock was their most valued possession.

Mechalke was part of a gang. One night he would visit the stable of one of his neighbors and take a horse or two. These he would deliver to a member of the gang who waited a short distance away. This second man brought them to a third, and the third to a fourth, until the horses were far away and could be safely sold at a fair. The horses were never brought to the same fair twice. In this way it seemed as if the animals disappeared magically.

One evening Mechalke brought a friend to join him in his drinking. The moment I noticed Kirk I was nervous. I was even more so when I saw Mechalke was treating and acting cheerful instead of being in his usual sullen mood. Every time Kirk got up to leave, Mechalke poured him another glass and found some more interesting things to talk about. It became late. Finally Kirk said, "I'm going home." Mechalke tried to rise too. He staggered about here and there and collapsed on the floor. Kirk gave a laugh and walked out.

When I was alone I looked at the lifeless heap of flesh lying on the floor. Suddenly it winked. Mechalke got up and returned to the table. The first thing he wanted was more brandy. As I set down the glass, he said with a grin, "You know what? Kirk's horses are already in Kremenets." I was not surprised as I had suspected all along he was keeping Kirk occupied while his partners took the horses.

I was hoping Mechalke would leave now and I would be free of him. But such hopes were in vain. He informed me that I was going to be his witness that he was here all night. To be safe he was going to spend the night with me. This was how it had been several times before, and once again, unwillingly, I was made an accessory to the gang.

It was exactly like the other times. He took my bed and in a second was comfortable and giving out thunderous snores. But I was too afraid to sleep at all. I paced back and forth. Suddenly I heard the sound of horses. Men came running to the door and pounded so hard, the wood started cracking. When I flung it open, in rushed Kirk, his brother Ilya, and five of their friends. "Where is Mechalke?" Ilya demanded in a loud voice. I pointed my finger to the corner. They began to consult with each other, and in the meantime, one of them gave me a push and screamed, "Hurry up and bring some brandy." I came running back with a bottle and some glasses. Kirk said, "My horses are gone." I did not know what to say. My face was burning. Finally I murmured, "God should help you track them down."

One of the peasants slammed his glass down. "We're wasting time. Come on. Let's wake Mechalke." They crowded about the sleeper. Kirk bent over and shouted in his ear, "Little father, wake up." Mechalke moaned a little and turned over. Now Ilya approached him and gave him a shove in the side and screamed, "You know where the horses are." Mechalke jerked and sat up with bulging eyes. Another peasant went over and pushed him down onto the floor, where Ilya kicked him in the head so hard that blood spurted out.

The servant girl was awakened by the commotion. Dressed only in her shift, her hair loose and flying about, she ran into the room and started screaming hysterically. I grabbed her by the arms and pushed her out. The whole time she struggled and scratched at my face. She was incredibly strong. I kept whispering to her over and over, "Go to your room and lock your door." Finally she understood I was trying to protect her. She ran into her room and did what I said.

I went back to the men. What I saw sickened me. They had grabbed Mechalke's feet and were dragging him back and forth across the room so that his head thumped against the floor. He was completely bloody and battered like a dead animal. Finally they dropped him. Ilya gave him one last kick in the head. One of the peasants cried, "Hey, he must be dead," and another, "We'll leave him with the Jew." They all ran out, one pushing another to be first to get to the horses and gallop away.

I was frantic. What should I do? I rushed out to the well for water. First I would wash the corpse—it sickened me to leave

Mechalke all bloody. Then I would run away. If I stayed I would be arrested and the peasants would testify that I was the murderer. I lugged in a bucket brimful of water and poured it over Mechalke. He began to moan. I got down on my knees and started slapping his cheeks. The man was not flesh but iron to still be alive. Shakily he stood up. He began to mumble in a confused way about the Virgin Mary. Suddenly he threw his arms about me. He kissed me all over my face and neck, blessed me and swore to be my eternal protector. His embraces were crushing my ribs and I had to cry out from the pain. Another moment and he would have broken all my bones, but fortunately he fainted. I was left to nurse the scratches on my face and the bruises all over the rest of me. I could not sleep at all. Not only the pains of my body kept me up, but I was terrified that the peasants would return.

In the morning I became aware that the servant was missing. She had run out of the house without my noticing and spent the night in the forest. When she came back she was shivering and kept screaming, "I am cold. I am cold." I saw to it that she went to bed and was covered up, but in a little while she became hot and began swelling. I fetched a peasant woman who lived nearby. She told me if I wanted the girl to live I should take a shirt and kerchief belonging to her and go to Anipolia the conjurer.

Mechalke had finally left, so I did what she said and went as quickly as possible. Anipolia lived in a small hut in the forest. A few others waited before me for advice, and I too had to wait. I could see through the open door a Russian woman confiding her problems. Anipolia whispered to herelf and then threw herself on the earth and wriggled about. I began to reproach myself; even though it was quite far, I should have gone for a doctor. Instead, because I was tired and frightened, I had obeyed the peasant woman. Now I was oppressed with the thought that the maid would die through my neglect.

Shortly I was called inside. Upon receiving several coins, the old woman, Anipolia, took a book, turned it round and round, and then opened a page and read in a simple Ukrainian, "A young woman went out in the night and caught a fever, but she will recover." Then she began to babble a language I could not under-stand. She took the scarf and shirt from me and I had to pay more money, and she had me gather leaves from the garden, which she sprinkled with water.

When I went home I was trembling. I kept hoping that like Mechalke, the girl would be resurrected. How astonished I was to see her running toward me from the distance. She was completely well.

Whether it was because of Mechalke's prayers or because Me-chalke himself was watching over me I do not know, but I lived safely through the autumn months. Not only that, but he promised that when my in-laws came back I wouldn't have to sell brandy anymore.

During this time I had several opportunities to visit the jail. I packed kosher food and took every pain to bring my relatives what they needed. I had to bring along a bottle of brandy also. I would say to the warder, "I have a bottle in my possession and I don't know what to do with it," and his answer was, "Give it to me. I'll know." Then he led me down a dark passage, opened a heavy oak door with a key, and left me alone in a half-dark, tiny room. This was an empty cell and there was an iron bed, a stool, and a wash-stand. After a while my family was brought to me. They had on green flannel dressing gowns, thick wool stockings, and boat-shaped yellow slippers that were so big they could barely walk. It was damp and cold there and we were all shivering. Both my in-laws had rheumatism; their life in prison made them irritable. My father-in-law did most of the talking. His hands would shake and he cried and moaned, *"Oy vey,* tragedy has overcome me." He was worried about being a pauper when he was released because so much money had been lost—the fine, the lawyer's fee, and the witness fees to the goyim who had turned them in to the author-ities. Sometimes I was told some ugly story about how they had been spat on or tormented in some other way because they were Jews. But usually no one talked to them. They did not even know what time it was, except for the ringing of church bells. They received no exercise, except once a week when they were let out into a small courtyard. All they saw there were thick, stone walls and the spire of a church.

My wife looked different; her skin was darker and she had lost some weight. She was too shy to tell me, but on one of my visits Malke spoke up. "*Nu,* congratulations David, you are going to be a father." I glanced over at Chaya and she was staring at the ground and I saw her face was burning. I did not know what to say. I would have been happy under normal conditions for such a blessing, but already the prison was having a poor effect on my wife's health. How could she endure a pregnancy? Maybe the child would be born deformed. Maybe it would be stillborn. On the day I received this announcement I left the prison with a heavy heart, and every day that followed I worried and felt sorrowful.

Finally I had the good news that they would be released from prison. I went to fetch them with a sled. We rode along in silence, all like strangers to each other—and it was true they hardly knew me. Yet it was strange because they had been a little friendlier when I visited them and I thought the moment they got out we would be a close family. Suddenly my mother-in-law said, "You didn't bring me the right kerchief to wear." I was surprised she would speak in such an angry tone over such a small thing. Then I thought that I could not expect them to act normally after such an experience as they had suffered and I must be patient. I apologized and Malke seemed satisfied.

When we got to the house Chaya went directly to the bedroom and closed the door. She felt tired and wanted to rest. I was left with the old people. They started looking things over, inside and out. They seemed so gloomy that I made an effort to cheer them up, but whenever I talked, they did not answer. I decided they must be tired like Chaya.

I said, "My dear parents, why don't you relax? I can take care of everything."

Moishe burst out, "How can I relax when I see how you ruined me?"

"What are you talking about?"

Then he began to complain that the garden did not look right, that I had let the supplies in the store run low. Everything was completely wrong. When I tried to protest, it made him angrier, so I just kept quiet. I looked over at Malke and saw she was agreeing with everything her husband said. And when my wife woke up from her nap, all she knew was that her parents were angry, so she should be too.

Even when we were alone I got from her looks full of suspicion and dislike that made me sick at heart. I went over and put my arms around her and felt her flinch. It was night, so without a word I went up to sleep in the attic. That was what the first day of reunion with my family was like.

How could I blame them? The prison had distorted their minds. They were full of shame and bitterness and all they cared about were appearances. From morning until night there were arguments. They attacked each other, but more often I was their victim. I decided to do everything I could think of to try to win their affection. My efforts completely failed. Moishe stopped using my name and began to address me as "ignoramus." How it was he picked the title that would most hurt, I do not know. It stung especially because here I was suffering in this remote place and one of my greatest desires was to meet someone with whom I could discuss books. I kept hoping that some Jew with children who lived in the vicinity would hire a tutor with whom I could become friends.

I remember I was thinking about this one Shabbes morning when Moishe and I were going to go to services a short distance away at a rich Hasid's. Malke and Chaya looked me over to see that my appearance was acceptable and immediately they began picking at me: "Your cravat is not tied properly." "Your suit is not buttoned right." "There's a piece of straw in your hair." When at last I met their approval, Moishe and I were allowed to leave. We walked through the forest. To all my attempts at conversation, he answered with a grunt. I gave up and just amused myself with my own thoughts. I even began to compose a fine speech on Torah in honor of Shabbes. Shortly my enthusiasm overcame me and I began to recite it aloud to Moshe. He silenced me at once: "Be quiet, ignoramus."

We came to a two-story wooden house inside a circle of fir trees. The house was in the peasant style, with decorative wood carvings along the eaves and around the windows. The weather was freezing cold and it was good to go inside where it was warmer. Several men were waiting for us; a few still had their coats and fur caps on and I kept mine on too because even though there was a fire going, I was chilled to the bone. I dreaded when I would have to go outside again. We had to wait for one more person. He arrived soon and we began to pray. When the services were over, I was still shivering. Moishe said to me, "Let's go home."

I pretended not to hear and gathered with the others to partake of some snacks our host's wife put out for us. There were some kreplach that really cheered me up. I liked the way the grease dripped out of them, and everyone was so merry that they did not care if their cuffs got soiled. They ate with appetite, and they drank too. I was basking in the warmth and friendliness of the others, but Moishe was impatient.

"Let's go before you make a fool of yourself," he whispered in my ear.

I said in a loud voice, "Is it polite to partake in such hospitality from someone and then leave without saying a few words of Torah in return?" I was quite intoxicated by now.

"My friends," I turned and addressed the group, "what is the difference between piety and orthodoxy? Allow me to share some of my thoughts. There are people who get up early each morning and go to the Bes Medresh to pray and recite blessings. They come home and do not drink without making a blessing and certainly do not eat before washing and then saying grace. They do not leave the house without first kissing the mezuzah on the door. When such a person performs all these things, he becomes an important person to the Creator of the Universe. For each of his acts he has an answer—a verse of Torah one time, washing his hands another, and prostrating himself to the ground yet another. This is orthodoxy.

"Piety is different. The first law of piety is to love your work and hate dishonesty. You must give people the right measurements and do not fool anyone. Do not pour water into brandy. Do not lie. Do not try to rent a store that someone else has been renting for years. And so on. I think 'Love your neighbor as yourself' is the summation of piety."

My companions congratulated me. My host, a fat man with golden skin, poured a brimming glass of brandy; a few drops even dripped over the lip of the glass. I downed it in a gulp. Everyone applauded. A few men began to dance and I joined them. In the corner sat Moishe glaring at me. All at once I realized he thought I addressed the speech especially to him. I decided I really needed to have a few more glasses.

When finally we left I was nearly dead drunk. Moishe dragged me along. I staggered and could hardly keep up. The liquor made me hot and I opened my coat. "Fool, you'll be sick," he said disgustedly. I started laughing. It struck me as hilarious that there was snow all around and I had been so cold before, but now I was warm. In this condition I arrived home. The minute we went inside Moishe pulled away from me and joined the committee of judgment which awaited me, my wife and mother-in-law. Also there were my two brothers-in-law, Yisroel and Eizy, who lived in nearby villages and had come for Shabbes. I was becoming better acquainted with them now that my in-laws were back from jail. I shouted at the top of my voice to them all, *"Gut Shabbes."*

The only one who answered was Eizy, the elder brother, a tall, strong man who was a little awkward in his manner. Eizy had always been a good friend and someone I admired. Even though he had five children whom he could barely support, he still tried to help others when he could. *"Gut Shabbes,* David," he replied and put his arm about me in order to lead me to the bedroom. "Come along, David. You'll rest. You'll feel better." Slowly we progressed across the room and I felt grateful to him for his gentleness.

The other brother, Yisroel, stood there stroking the long *peyes* he wore down to his shoulders to show by their length how pious he was. It seems he was disappointed that my drunkenness was being passed over so lightly. He taunted his sister, "Chaya, this is the best husband you could get?" My wife, who was in her sixth month of pregnancy and was not feeling well, burst into tears. Although I was drunk, I believe I am right when I say there was a look of triumph in Yisroel's eyes. From the beginning he had been stirring up trouble between my in-laws, my wife, and myself.

Such fury swept through me that if Eizy had not held my hands, I would have hit Yisroel. I started screaming at him, "Why do you hate me so much? Is it because when we went to visit the rebbe at Alik together I got a whole fish for *shrayim** and you only got a crumb? Is that crumb still sticking in your throat? Or maybe it's because I was asked to be *hazzan* at services and people praised me for singing well. These small things you can't tolerate."

While I was saying this, Yisroel laughed shrilly. My wife rushed to her mother's arms and Moishe came up to me with upraised threatening fists. I would have received many blows from my father-in-law if Eizy had not shielded me with his body and pulled me into the next room. There he put me into bed and covered me over with a thick quilt. My head was spinning round and round, and soon I was asleep.

I awoke with a burning throat and knew I would be sick, as Moishe had predicted. I got up and dragged myself out to the family. I was in a contrite mood and longed for a friendly glance but met only stony stares. Malke could not control herself. "It's not enough you're a thickhead, but a drunkard besides."

Her words proved prophetic. I went from swallowing all their insults to swallowing liquor as well. When my relations started to nag at me I would take one cup, then two, three, or more—as much as I needed to forget.

Things went from bad to worse. I saw Chaya was suffering as she neared the time of her delivery. Her legs were so swollen she could barely walk. I knew that whenever she was alone, she cried. Her eyes were always red. She was terrified of the day she would be confined, but how could I comfort her? Part of her sorrow was that she had married me. The sicker my wife felt, the more my in-

---

* Food that a Hasidic rabbi has left over on his plate after a meal which is distributed to his followers as signs of his esteem.

laws harassed me, as if it were my fault. I was not even feeling well myself. I had a really bad cold, and a cough remained with me. Sometimes I spit blood, but I never said anything to them about it. I just tried to continue with my life, go on as before, but the strain was becoming unbearable for me.

I thought of that time I was trapped in the pit with the dogs barking around me and ready to bite—my life was like that. Even in Zakit it had been better. No one had tormented me. The only respite I had was the few times I traveled to see my father and my younger brothers.

I felt my mind was deteriorating. Once I had been considered clever, and now I was always dull. I walked around in a stupor and was only shrewd about finding opportunities to drink.

I did notice that the peasants acted friendlier to me. It was because they pitied me! And the one who was kindest was the priest. Whenever the priest saw me, he gave me a look that I understood well—it was the sympathy of a fellow sufferer. At least my wife did not chase her husband with a broom the way his did.

One day I found him staggering along the road, stunned by one of her blows. I put my arm about him and assisted him to walk. It occurred to me that it would not be appropriate for people to see us arm in arm, and so I took him to a place in the forest where it would be unusual for anyone to pass.

I happened to have a bottle of brandy in my coat pocket and offered him some. He took a swallow gratefully.

"If you ever need my assistance, ask me," he told me.

"Many thanks," I said.

We sat on a log. Spring had finally arrived; bees buzzed around, and big white butterflies fluttered in the air. Both of us were reluctant to leave. He started talking about his childhood. His parents had died when he was ten and the monks at a monastery raised him. This was an unusual arrangement. He made himself so useful that they kept him on. The monastic life suited him.

"Why did they force me to marry? I'm not like these peasants here, and they don't like me." Tears rolled down his cheeks.

On other occasions we met and tried to console each other.

* * *

One day it seemed I was going to have a small break from the daily routine. The store needed fresh supplies. Moishe did not feel well enough to travel to town for them at this time, and Malke would not leave Chaya. They delayed for a week and finally decided they were going to take a big chance and entrust the task of making the purchases to the "ignoramus."

They told me to go to Viliya for the supplies, but I went to Dubno instead because there I could meet my uncle Nutah. I could buy the supplies at his store; also I could stay overnight with him instead of with strangers.

It turned out to be a pleasant visit. I was welcomed into a household that had the warmth and love that my own lacked. My uncle, a small, white-haired man, was a widower with three lively daughters. The eldest had a peppery tongue. I had to be alert to answer all her questions. I saw she liked a quick retort, something to make her and her sisters laugh. The second sister was learned for a woman. I was impressed by the number of books she had read. In the youngest, Leah, a delicate child, I saw a good and pure soul. She fussed over her father to see he was comfortable, but Uncle Nutah and the others, in turn, seemed to keep constant watch over her.

I was informed that a few years before, Leah had been sick and near death. When she recovered Uncle Nutah made up a song. The evening I spent with them he sang it for me. I found it simple and charming.

> *I traveled over the mountains and over the valleys,*
> *Until I got to the Kiev hospital.*
> *And when the doctors said the chances were poor for my child,*
> *God sent me the Angel Raphael,*
> *And she recovered.*

When I heard my uncle had been in Kiev, I became interested and asked him to relate some of his experiences. He told me about a poor, sick woman who had been there at the same time he was. The woman had traveled about to different doctors, but nowhere did she receive a cure. Everyone said she must go to Kiev. Even though she had no money, she managed to go there and brought along her infant son. The doctors at the medical school informed her she needed an operation immediately, so she went around begging people to pay the hospital fees, and also to take care of her child until she recovered. No one would help. Instead they laughed at her and told her she should return to her village. This was impossible because not only did she lack the fare, but she was too weak to travel. In a few days her condition had become so bad that she felt she was near death. When night came she wrapped her child in a blanket and left him in the street because she could no longer care for him. The Russian caretaker who goes about the city lighting the lamps found him and brought him to the priest. Word went out that the boy was to be baptized. Immediately the Jews of Kiev raised an enormous ransom to retrieve the child. Now they decided to take care of the child and also make sure the mother received the operation she needed.

Because my uncle was generous himself, he had little patience with the lack of charity in others, and he concluded his story by saying, "Wouldn't it have been better if they had helped her in the first place?"

We stayed up conversing late into the night, and when I did go to bed my nerves were not jangling as if they had been pecked at by crows. I did not need any brandy. I could go to sleep right away.

The next morning I went to Uncle Nutah's store and he sold me the supplies, and at a considerable savings for my father-in-law. I loaded them on the wagon and could have left Dubno, but I decided to walk around a little. I guess I wanted to delay going home as long as possible because to me it was like returning to hell.

I went into one shop where there was a dispute taking place. A man named Simcha was leaving for America the next month and his friends were arguing over whether he was doing the right thing. The discussion went back and forth.

"Simcha, you can still cash in the ticket. Even in America Jews starve. Why go so far? Why throw away the little you have?"

"Don't listen, you'll make your fortune there . . . and I hear the government in America lets the Jews breathe some of the air. It's not forbidden."

"How do you know conditions won't improve in Russia? The wheel always turns. Don't be an idiot."

Everyone raised his voice and expressed his opinion, except for me. I was too upset. My heart was thudding hard. I walked out of there as if in a dream. America. Why hadn't I gone there when Simcha Godels told me? Here there were no opportunities. Maybe I would have a chance there. An evil voice counseled me, "Just run away. Your wife hates you. It's too bad about the baby, but Chaya and her parents will take care of it. You're on a downhill road here, and the child should not be raised with a worthless father." I wandered around the town trying to get these ideas out of my head. The thought of how I had hurt my mother because of my own selfishness sobered me. No, I would face up to my responsibilities.

I went into another shop. Here I was the only customer. The storekeeper was a fat man with an apron around his waist.

"Why do you look so gloomy? Here, cheer yourself up. Taste this cracker." He took one from an open carton. Behind him in a second room I saw hundreds of similar cartons stacked up. I bit into it, and it was delicious.

"Where did you get these?"

"These crackers are called galetas. In 1888 when the big military maneuvers took place which Czar Alexander himself attended, all supplies passed through Dubno. When the maneuvers were over, a thousand boxes of these galetas were left behind and I bought them up. Do me a favor and have another—one less I have to worry about."

I liked them so much I took two more and as I was chewing, an idea suddenly flashed through my mind. If I were able to make a profitable business deal, my relations in Tureni might be better pleased with me. Perhaps this was the opportunity to change our life together for the better.

"How much do you charge a box?"

"I'll sell at a loss—only three rubles."

Immediately I started calculating how much I could charge the peasants and what the profit would be. In Dubno, where there were several stores, the crackers did not sell, but in Tureni, where goods were scarce, I was certain the crackers could be sold at five rubles a box, or even more.

I said, "I'll take two hundred."

The storekeeper shook my hand vigorously and looked overjoyed.

I put down a fifty-ruble deposit, loaded as many of the boxes as I could on my wagon, and told the storekeeper I would come back for the rest later. Then I drove off for Tureni.

I could not have been more mistaken about what Moishe and Malke would think about my business deal. When I came home and they discovered I had ordered two hundred boxes of galetas, they started to really torture me. Malke cried, "Trouble has found us again. Plague has overcome us. We go from one tragedy into another."

I tried to calm her. "If you don't want the rest, it's only fifty rubles lost."

"Those fifty rubles should grow on your conscience and weigh you down to the earth."

My in-laws followed me about, screaming, cursing, and wishing the most horrible torments for me. They would have gone on without stop, but it happened to be a Friday and the sun was setting. Shabbes had arrived, so we needed to light the candles and pray.

My wife had been hiding in the bedroom to stay away from all this turmoil, but now she came out. I sang the Sabbath song *"Eshet Chayil"* from the proverbs of Solomon. The words were:

> *A woman of worth.*
> *Who can find her?*
> *For her price is far above rubies.*
> *The heart of her husband trusteth in her.*

As I sang I glanced over at Chaya and I hoped she would note my misery and I would see some pity in her eyes. She looked as if she wanted to spit in my face. What a contrast there was between the atmosphere of my uncle's home and my own.

The Shabbes meal, which is supposed to be beautiful and peaceful, was one of misery. I said nothing, just looked from face to face. Their words pounded into my brain like hammers.

"Why did you send him when you knew he was an idiot?"

"What is the difference between an ignoramus and a pregnant woman? A woman pushes out her own stomach, but a fool punches out someone else's."

"*Nu*, my daughter, you fell in over your ears and you are a pain to your parents."

I went to bed in the attic, and the next day I tried to keep to myself. On Sunday morning I got up early and went directly to the store. Several things had become clear in my mind. One was that I was going to leave them; the other was that before I ran away, I was going to prove the galetas would sell. Peasants started arriving after the church services. I gave them samples of the crackers and they said they tasted delicious. Within two hours every box was sold. My relations had noticed the peasants carrying the boxes from the store. Now they came running in as if nothing had happened between us.

"David, where are all the boxes?"

"You see they were all sold."

"All sold? You must go to Dubno and get the rest as soon as possible," my father-in-law ordered me. He was so excited, his eyes had a wild look.

Malke whined, "Why didn't you buy for my Yisroel? He could use them at his store." Eizy's store she did not mention.

For a few moments I could not even speak. I must have turned white; the peasants were staring with astonishment. Finally I said to my in-laws, "You dogs. No wonder Gerson died prematurely. You devour a human being. I won't do business for you. I'll bring nothing for you. A little while ago the only title you had for me was 'drunkard' or 'ignoramus.' Now suddenly I have value. Don't talk to me again."

My father-in-law appeared stunned. He looked at me as if he

were seeing me for the first time, that I was a human being also. He wanted to tell me something, but I did not wait to hear.

I ran out and went walking in the forest. I pushed through the brush and it scratched my hands and face, but I hardly noticed. I had slept poorly the night before and I felt so exhausted that I could not think clearly. Every few minutes I had to stop to cough, and it shook my whole frame. It felt as if my insides were about to pour out of me. I was so upset that I was talking aloud to myself and arguing with my dead mother. "You see they're killing me. Just like Gerson. What am I to do?"

I started coughing violently again and fell down on the ground, and when I recovered I did not feel like getting up. Let that be my grave. I lay there a long time, half-dozed, finally felt chilled to my bones, and decided to drag myself back.

Eizy was waiting for me on the porch. Moishe had sent a peasant to fetch him. In this way a little consideration was shown for my feelings because Eizy was the only one with whom I was willing to talk. As usual he greeted me kindly. Then he tried to plead for his parents and sister, that they acted badly but I should forgive them because of what they suffered in jail.

"They are truly sorry, and as a Jew you have to accept a sincere apology and forgive them."

I felt too sick to argue with him. Finally I said, "Leave me alone. I'm going to Dubno to buy the rest of the boxes."

He saw it was no use to stop me. I went and hitched the horse to the wagon. Just as I was climbing into the driver's seat, Malke came out of the house with a timid manner, but her words enraged me: "Please buy for Yisroel."

I lashed at the horse and left. The trip was a nightmare for me. Sweat was pouring out of me and a stabbing pain went through my head. Several times I thought I would faint. Yet I was driven on, could not turn back. When I got to Dubno I dragged myself into the shop and asked to buy additional boxes. The storekeeper answered that he had raised the price to double. I just took the rest of the original order of two hundred boxes.

Even though it was getting late, I decided to drive back. I had no control over my actions. First I was going to stop at Eizy's village. When I got to his house it was the middle of the night. I roused his wife from bed and delivered all the boxes to her for Eizy's store. She was frightened at the way I was behaving. She asked me if I wanted to sleep there because it was better not to travel in darkness, and also I looked sick to her. I did not even find it necessary to answer her. I climbed back on the wagon and drove away. My only thought was that when I got home, I would go inside while they were asleep, pack together a few things, and run away. I remembered the conversation I heard in the shop in Dubno. Probably I would go to America. The way I felt, the further, the better. They should never find me, and I should forget everything.

I was astonished that a lamp was burning and all of them— Malke, Moishe, Chaya, and Eizy—were waiting up for me. The moment the wagon came into the yard they ran outside. I looked at Chaya with her swollen stomach and thought how she was carrying a child I would never see. It made my heart ache. They started coming toward me, talking. It was like a buzzing; I did not hear a word. I shouted as loud as I could, "Leave me alone; don't dare talk to me." Moishe put his arms out and caught me just as I fainted.

They carried me inside and put me to bed. Of all that happened right after this I have only a faint memory. I was barely conscious for several days. My in-laws were afraid that I would die and leave a widow and orphan. Now they showed a completely different side to their characters. Moishe got up every day before dawn and prayed over me. Malke tended me selflessly. She was an excellent nurse, and without her constant care I probably would have died. A peasant came and showed her how to brew a remedy to rub on my chest. It took several hours to make it and had to be prepared fresh each day, but she did it without fail. The moment I gained consciousness, she and Moishe came over, got down on their knees, and begged me for my forgiveness. I did not like to see the old people with bowed heads like that. I told them to get up, that we should forget everything that happened in the past.

It took me a long time to recuperate. At first I stayed in bed and could hardly lift my head. Later I was able to sit in a chair for fifteen minutes, then a half-hour. Now that I was better I saw some sign of my father-in-law's distaste returning in a word or gesture. These were habits from which he could not escape. But always when this happened he stopped himself and looked miserable and sorry. My mother-in-law was different. She had become a devoted admirer of mine. Malke had come to realize her future rested with me because I was the one most likely to provide for her old age and Moishe's. Once she was for you, nothing you did was wrong. Now I was her favorite son. It reminded me of when Aunt Bobbah reconciled herself to me.

One time Yisroel came in and made his usual sarcastic comments to me. Malke gave him some sharp looks, but he continued to believe it was his privilege to be rude to others. The result was that my mother-in-law chased him out of the house. The next time he came he saw he better hold his tongue in my presence or she would attack him with all the venom she used to reserve for me. He had to content himself with stroking his sidelocks, and they had grown so long, that that was all you noticed about him.

I came out of this illness a much harder person. I was only eighteen years old, but I felt older. The freshness of youth was gone from me.

⇜9

A son is acquired and I am lost

IN THE SPRING, Chaya was delivered of a healthy child, a boy. I
was still weak and could hardly walk, but of course the *bris** could
not be delayed but had to take place on the eighth day after the
birth, which was a Friday. There was no *mohel†* in the vicinity to
perform it, and so one from Viliya was used. His name was Lezier
and he was a rich man who did it as an act of charity. Usually he
brought with him gifts of food, clothing, and money for the
mother, and the poorer she was, the more he gave. To villages like
Tureni he also brought along additional Jews to make up the necessary *minyan.*

On Friday our guests assembled. First came Yisroel, a little less
sour than usual since there were going to be some strangers to im-
press. Eizy came also, with his family. He bent over his new
nephew making all kinds of gurgling sounds, and Chaya was
beaming. Lezier arrived with four companions. These four, plus
Lezier, Moishe, Yisroel, Eizy, and myself made nine. But a tenth
male was needed. Shabbes had already begun, so we said the

---

* Circumcision.
† Person who is authorized to perform a circumcision.

prayers and then waited around. We dared not perform the *bris* without a *minyan*, but where could we find another Jew? Midnight came. Lezier said he would go outside a moment for a breath of air. Suddenly we heard a joyous cry. Lezier had seen an old Jew, a peddler with a pack on his back, coming out of the forest. He rushed over to him and begged him to come to the *bris*. The old man said, "That is my favorite occasion," and consented.

Immediately my son was brought forward. My wife held him tightly while the *bris* was performed. The baby began to shriek in pain. Chaya tried to comfort him, while my in-laws started getting some refreshments ready. Everyone gathered, but it was noted that the peddler was gone. With the exception of myself, the men rushed outside and began to search for him. He had disappeared into the forest without a trace.

When Lezier returned with the others he said not a word but went over to my son, bowed, and kissed his forehead reverently. Then he turned and addressed us, "Others may doubt it, but I believe wholeheartedly that the prophet Elijah has been to visit and given this child his blessing."

The days went by, then weeks and then months. The life was very much like that at Zakit. My relations were treating me better, including my wife. With Chaya it was not because I had been so sick, but because we had a child. Constantly she was bent over his cradle, studying his face. It was good for her to care for such a helpless creature; it gave her more confidence and she was less constrained in her manner.

I started to notice that when she suckled the baby she liked to sit beside me. The love our son inspired in her was wide enough to include me also. In her quiet way, she began to show me attentions I had never received before—a kind or respectful look, some small job I was supposed to do that I found already finished by her hand, once a gift of a flower left on my pillow. It was easier to talk and sometimes I even tried to joke with her. She smiled and a certain light came into her eyes. If I went away for a few hours, when I returned Chaya would be waiting for me on the road. I knew she had missed me.

I appreciated all this. I should have been happy, but there was a darkness on my spirit always weighing me down. One day I discovered that the few books I possessed, which I had stored away in a place in the wall, had been eaten up by termites. I felt bitter. Why had I studied and prepared myself for a different life, only to have it destroyed the way the books had been? I was lonely and without a companion with whom I could really talk. Even someone like Eizy brought no comfort; I would try to share my ideas with him, but he could not grasp them, and it always ended with me feeling disappointed. I started to feel lethargic and became absent-minded and distant to people. In a way the fights with my in-laws had served some purpose; they kept away a little the depression that was overtaking me because I lived in this desolate place. I hated it more and more and felt that I was buried alive.

I traveled to the Alik rabbi several times to confide in him. At first he tried to pacify me. Then he saw how deep my dissatisfaction was and he said, "The Talmud commands us, if we cannot make a livelihood in one place to move to another." His words did not apply directly to my situation, but they were such that after this I frequently pondered them. The rabbi had seen into my heart, that it embittered me that I had to rely on my in-laws for my work. I wanted to be independent and earn my living for myself and my wife and child with my own two hands.

No longer did I consider running off by myself. Now, above all things, I was committed to my family. But it was a period of great doubt for me. Should I accept conditions and try to live with them, or should I, Chaya, and Aaron leave Tureni? Would Chaya consent? Where should we go?

The situation in Russia seemed dismal to me. Everywhere there were pogroms, and often the police assisted in harming the Jews. From one public official came the statement "The real crime is to interfere with the moral indignation of the public against the Jewish vermin."

So maybe it was best to go to America; but when I reflected on it, I couldn't make up my mind to do that either. It would be hard to uproot ourselves; maybe there would be an improvement in conditions here. After all, the brief reign of Alexander II had been an enlightened period when life was better for all. Unfortunately, in 1881, this czar who had freed the serfs was assassinated. But maybe another good czar would come to power.

Should we go or not? How would it be accomplished? These questions and others were always with me, even tormented me in my sleep. It never felt comfortable to discuss it with my wife. I struggled alone with my unhappiness. I wanted so desperately some change in my own life that when something important happened in the outside world—Nicholas II came to power—it affected me deeply. I cried when I heard there was a new czar. I hoped a new leader would show justice to our people, and this was the hope of all Jews.

Hindah's brother-in-law was in the military at this time, and he came to visit me and described how the Jewish soldiers who served with him celebrated the coronation. They decided that each one would contribute a ruble, and with the money a Torah scroll would be bought and a *shul* rented, and there a special blessing for the czar could be made. The garrison chief granted them permission to do this, and on the day of the coronation they began outside the city and solemnly paraded toward the *shul.* They bore a canopy, and the Torah was carried beneath it. The best singers among them walked together and sang in Hebrew, "God give aid to the King."

In the weeks after the coronation I felt some optimism. To me it seemed that opportunities might open up for Jews all over Russia, and that a better fate might be awaiting me.

Two years passed in Tureni and nothing happened in this forsaken village. Then suddenly a decree was issued that parcels of trees in the forest would be auctioned. To us this seemed a good turn of fortune because suddenly the village was filled with speculators, officials, and men looking for work. They all needed supplies and purchased them from Moishe. It seemed he would be wealthy. I, too, was earning extra money. Being familiar with the forest, I was able to act as a guide, showing people about the forest and explaining which trees were sound. An official was so impressed that he obtained for me a government position with the title of "lumber specialist."

Then came a second decree, that all Jews living in our village had to leave immediately. Tureni had never seemed to me the most ideal place, but now that we were being asked to leave, I saw it was the only home we had. I went to the bailiff and explained that my wife was born here and my father-in-law lived here forty years. I asked that we be considered exceptions. My petition was forwarded to the governor and was refused.

The same official who recommended me for the position of lumber specialist spoke up for me again and said I was essential. They gave me a visa to stay—but only me. Malke and Moishe went to live with Eizy, and my wife and son went to Yisroel's. My wife did not fare well at her brother's. He had persuaded me to pay for the construction of a small cottage in his yard for Chaya. As soon as it was completed he evicted his sister and she had to stand on the road with the baby in her arms and all her possessions scattered around. I'll never forget how she looked when I went to fetch her. She stared straight ahead, her face white, while the baby screamed. Her pain was so great that she could not bring herself to comfort our child. I tried to take him from her, but she would not let me. While I gathered her suitcases, she climbed on the wagon. The rocking motion put the child to sleep and we drove in silence.

I was reminded of that time we came back from the prison, because Chaya had the same drooping, sorrowful look to her. It had taken a long time to recover from what she suffered in jail, and I wondered what the result would be of Yisroel's heartlessness. The edict that tore her away from her home in Tureni was a terrible shock to her, but that a brother could be so cruel was even worse.

I took her to stay with Eizy and went to visit her frequently. Whenever I came, she always seemed sober and grave, always had a prayer book in her hand. She was becoming an exceptionally God-fearing person. Every ritual had to be performed precisely— this was where she found her main solace at this time, not in her husband.

* * *

It took a year of zealous effort on my part before my bribes came to the right person. I could not do anything for my in-laws, but the regime permitted Chaya and my son, Aaron, to rejoin me in Tureni. The village to which they returned was completely changed. The forest was devastated and the river clogged with logs. Trees which had been standing for hundreds of years were cut up into logs and floated down the Uhren to railroad depots or ports, and from there the wood was exported to Germany and England.

The village swarmed with strangers, men who ventured into the forest in the hope of making their fortunes. Most found tragedy instead. One had his leg crushed by a tree and another lost his hand by an ax blow. Two partners, their pockets loaded with money, were so confident of their good fortune that they risked riding over thin ice. The ice cracked and they fell into the water. I was in the rescue party that tried to reach them, but even with help in sight they could not hold on longer. They sank, along with their thousands of rubles.

Each day I heard of some new horror which sickened me, but the worst one was when a mass grave of thirty men was discovered. A Polish porter would wait at the railway station with his wagon and offer the cheapest rate to the lumber brokers who wanted to come to the forest to purchase wood. When they were far from any witness, he slaughtered his victims with an ax and took their money.

After witnessing such things, I decided that this was no atmosphere in which to raise a family and that it would be better to leave.

I was beginning to think more and more seriously of immigrating. The new czar, upon whom I had rested so much faith, proved himself to be a fanatical anti-Semite. The Jews were blamed for everything, including revolutionary activity among Russians. As many pogroms as there had been before, now there were more. All the old myths were revived, and once again Jews were arrested on charges of ritual killing. Frequently I heard news of new expulsions of Jews and of new anti-Semitic edicts; it seemed it was possible that the regime wanted to annihilate the Jewish population, and the result was that thousands of Jews were fleeing Russia.

I took the first step to achieving my escape. I talked it over with Chaya.

She rebuked me with great heat. "If a Jew suffers here on earth, he should think about God and the other world, not about America. Only criminals and selfish people go there."

It was clear it would take time for her to become accustomed to the idea, so for the time being I decided to say nothing more.

Meanwhile my own determination was increasing. Stories came to me continually of people whom I respected who had decided to emigrate, or of those who were already there and had become successful. My wife seemed to hear only of the failures. Her attitudes were like those of the peasants among whom we lived. You were never supposed to move; you always had to stay in the same place, no matter what. Perhaps if I had not traveled around and lived in Proskurov and Kishinev, and other places, I would have felt as she did.

"See how people perish in America," Chaya said to me one day and told me about a cousin of hers who went there and whose two children took sick and died.

I answered with ardor, "People prosper there too. In the case you mention, maybe worse things would have happened if the family had stayed in Russia. It is far better for someone to take a chance than to remain and become embittered."

At this time I had begun to earn a livelihood by buying and selling trees, and the experiences I had had in this business affected me deeply, adding to all my other dissatisfactions. This was how it was: A Russian landowner would arrive, and I went out doffing my cap and gave him an obeisant welcome. I led him into the house. He sat while I stood. As we discussed how much lumber he wished to buy, he would remark, "Jews are swindlers and they turn our good people into thieves." I had to listen and say nothing. When I went to collect what was owed to me, it was likely this same landowner would set his dogs on me, so that I had to run away and was never paid. What was worse, if I saw the landowner again, I felt compelled to take my cap off to him, just like a serf.

This slavishness was repulsive to me. When I was younger I could brush away the insults I endured as a Jew, but not now. Every abuse, every contemptuous glance, stung me, and I was burning up alive. I kept thinking about the advice of the Alik rabbi. I knew that if ever I came to a land where I did not have to doff my cap, I would bend down on my knees and kiss the earth.

To me it had finally become very clear that sooner or later we were going to have to leave, and meanwhile we were just wasting time. Wouldn't it be better to arrive in a new country while we were still young and had our strength? I did all I could to persuade Chaya. When she saw how earnest I was, she was horrified. "Are you so heartless, you want to rip me away from my parents?" Chaya was timid, afraid of anything unfamiliar. She dreamed one night she was on the ship crossing the Atlantic Ocean and she drowned, and she was convinced the dream was prophetic. She heard that Jews lost their religion in America, and this increased her antagonism to the idea. Even if she survived the crossing, how could such a pious person as herself live among idolators?

No matter how patient I was, I saw I could not move her. My efforts only made her more stubborn. We began to bicker constantly, and finally I saw that I had better hold my tongue, because whatever tenderness existed between us was being destroyed.

My feelings were locked inside me. In the beginning I wanted to leave because I hated my life here, but now I started to fall in love with this America, this unknown land. I had to have some object upon which to place all my hopes and dreams. In my mind it was a place of deliverance, a place where Jews could build a new and free life. I wanted my son to grow up there, and it hurt me to see Aaron's childhood going by. I comforted myself that Chaya was bound to see things as I did eventually. To me, small as it was, there was still hope. I only needed to be patient.

Something happened that brought things to a crisis between my wife and me. A calamity befell me. I was arrested and brought to trial for swindling. I had sold a peasant a few oaks. He carried them home through a forest belonging to an official and was accused of having stolen them from this forest. The peasant protested that he had bought them from me, so a subpoena was issued for my arrest on the charge that I had conspired with him to cover up the theft. The only thing that saved me was that the village priest went to court and testified on my behalf, and this impressed the judge favorably. Otherwise I would have had a long jail sentence.

When I came home from court I was quivering with resentment. There was no justice in this land for a Jew. If I wasn't sent to jail this week, in another month or a year it could very well happen. What difference did it make that I tried to follow a righteous path, that I always dealt honestly with people? I said to Chaya, "Now you see there are no successes for us here. Let us go to America." After I had barely escaped being sent to jail, her answer astonished me.

"We discussed this before and I told you I won't go." She sat with her arms folded tightly and looked away from me. To me it was as if she had closed up her ears.

I shouted at the top of my voice, "What else must happen before you see?"

"Don't gnaw my heart out."

She got up to walk away so I could not talk to her anymore. I grabbed her by the shoulders and began to shake her. Her head was snapping back and forth, her mouth open in horror, her eyes wild. Never had I laid hands on her like this before. My arms fell to my sides like weights. I saw she was trying to scream, but no sound came out. Finally she hissed like a snake, "What is America, your sweetheart? Your beloved?"

"If I cared less, you'd consent."

"I'd never consent!"

"Anything I want, you hate. . . . Just because I want . . ."

"Never. . . . You're never going . . . never . . . never . . ."

My hand rose and slapped her, leaving a red streak that spread across her pale cheek. She pulled away from me and burst into tears. And still it was not ended. We had to curse and say terrible things that should never have passed our lips.

The next day we were ashamed to look at each other. I went

about the house with guilty, averted eyes. All my illusions were swept away. I was convinced now that Chaya would never give way. A despairing feeling descended on me. In the afternoon I was on the way to visit one of my customers. As I walked along, my mind went over different scenes from my boyhood. I thought of myself riding the Arabian over the steppes in Bessarabia. Suddenly I began to weep and could not stop. I knew I would never experience that kind of freedom again.

I became constantly restless. I could hardly concentrate on anyone else's conversation. When I was in a room, it was like a cage. I paced back and forth. My stomach was tight as a knot and I could hardly sleep. Even if I drank some brandy, I would wake up an hour later, after its effects had worn off. My mood was a grim one and I had few hopes. I felt all my efforts would be thwarted. And it was at this time that I began to be a successful businessman.

This gave Chaya a lot of satisfaction. It was not only the extra money that pleased her, but that all the grave tragedies I had predicted had not come about. On the contrary, I was always lucky. I bought trees, had them milled, sold the lumber, and then reinvested. By risking every kopeck I had, I started making the kinds of deals a rich man would.

Finally I had enough capital to buy a large parcel of trees. Brokers were to come the next day to bid on sections of it. I decided to spend the evening going over my account book so that I would have all my costs memorized.

It was a warm summer evening and all was quiet. Aaron was asleep. Chaya sewed a little, brought me a cup of tea, and finally settled down with her prayer book. I checked the figures several times, and it was nearly time to go to bed.

I looked up at Chaya and I saw she was sitting with her body erect and a strained look on her face. She sniffed the air. I said, "What's the matter?"

"Shh . . ." Then she whispered, "Do you hear?" It was a low, grumbling sound. We both just stared at each other. I'll never forget the feeling of misery that passed between us. Even before we went out and saw the flames in the distance, we knew what it was.

I got shovels and we rushed to the part of the forest that was burning. We thought we could dig trenches and prevent the fire from spreading; several peasants were already doing that. It was hopeless. Everything was vanquished by the flames. I saw how an entire forest burns. The fire caught at the base of a tree and flew to the topmost branches. The whole parcel of trees I had bought was destroyed and much more as well. I was ruined. Now I saw it was my fate to be a pauper, just like my father.

The fire continued for a day and a half. When finally it had quenched itself, I went to look over the charred remains. Everything was smoking and black. In those dead ashes were all the ambitions I had had for a better life. I began to weep for myself, my wife, and my child. All we could anticipate was suffering.

Chaya came to join me, and her expression was stern. She said, "You will go to America."

"Now you send me . . . now, when we have nothing. Where will I get money for the fare?"

"I'll get it."

The next day she disappeared and I was alarmed. I did not know where to look for her. I went to Eizy's; I thought she might be there with her parents, but I did not find her. So I came home. About an hour later she came in looking exhausted. Without a word she went to the table, untied a kerchief, and spilled out some bills and coins. "Where did you get these?"

At first she would not answer, but then she said, "I went to the Devil for it."

She had gone to Kiniv to her brother Yisroel. She demanded he pay back the money he took from me to construct the cottage. Yisroel whined and said he had no money at all. Chaya replied, "I am going to go around to everyone and expose you as the hard-hearted and selfish person you are." He saw she was determined and he went to his overflowing cash box and extracted a little money. My wife asked him for more so the whole family could leave together, but for such a large amount she could not threaten

Yisroel. He would prefer to lose his reputation. He would prefer to cut off his long *peyes*. She had to settle for the sum that was sufficient for my fare.

I never thanked Chaya, only silently. In my thoughts she was elevated above what she had been before. I realized what her visit with her brother cost her. Just to behold him was terrible, but more so to ask him for something. She had to see how he squirmed about and detested him more; she had to fight him for something which deep in her heart she was against. The money she brought me so bitterly rescued me, gave me a new chance in life. But to Chaya, America was still fearful. Any sign of rejoicing on my part, or if I expressed gratitude, would have caused her pain.

Yet I had to prepare for the trip, and she could not be spared this.

I wrote to all alive that I was leaving for America. People came with advice, with envy that I was fortunate enough to have a chance in a new country, and with dire warnings. I was going to take a coach to Poland, and from there to take a train to Antwerp, and then book passage on a ship. I was told I would be lucky if I survived a trip across the ocean in steerage. Nothing could dissuade me. What choice did I have?

I knew no one in America, but soon I had a list of people to look up. Someone even gave me Mendel's name, if I cared to renew the acquaintance. It seems he was working as a pimp in New York. The matchmaker from Shumsk came to see me and gave me a letter for a nephew of his in Brooklyn. I found out what had happened to the girls to whom I had almost been betrothed. Miriam's father had died of a stroke, and soon after she married. Esther remained unwed. I was loaded down with gifts—some to deliver to others, and some for me. Yeshovua Greenshpan gave me a feather quilt. Eizy gave me a book of English phrases. My relatives from Proskurov were generous too, and gave me some fine cloth. Aunt Bobbah screamed and cried, and said I was ripping her heart out by leaving her. When I mentioned I would like her to look out for my wife, she acted a little cooler. Several years had gone by, but how could she forget the insults she had to bear at my wedding?

It was to Eizy I entrusted my wife and son until I could arrange passage for them. I knew I could rely on his kindness. The burdens I gave him were even heavier than I first realized. Chaya informed me she was pregnant. I felt as if a knife was stabbing me in the heart, but I did not reveal my pain. I said, "My wife, now you see there is more reason to go than ever, for the sake of this new child."

I saw the old anger flash in Chaya's eyes. "And if America gobbles you up? So many others have disappeared and left their wives *agunahs.*"

To reassure her seemed impossible. These doubts burned her; I saw it in the fervent manner in which she prayed, or in those moments when she suddenly took Aaron in her arms and hugged him so tightly that he struggled to get away. She would have to wait until the tickets were in her hands to stop suspecting me.

I went to my in-laws to beg them to convince her that I would not abandon her. They had a small room in Eizy's crowded house. They stayed there quietly as if they had been pushed aside from all of life. Moishe was in poor health, and when he greeted me it was from bed where he lay with his beard on top of the quilt. Malke sat beside him with her hands folded. They did not even light a lamp, but preferred to be in darkness. From the moment I entered the room, all they could talk about was their bitter hatred for the regime. They had never recovered from losing their home in their old age. When I started to talk about America, my father-in-law shouted, "Go. Go to America. Get out while there's time. Everything will burn here, not just the forest."

His furious words rang in my ears as ones of prophecy. As I traveled about to say good-bye to people for the last time, my eyes were quick to pick out what was sick or decaying. My poor father lay now, day and night, on a bench in the Bes Medresh. Devorah had been the instrument to bring about the final stroke of his fate. She sent the younger boys to a cousin and chased my father out. Now he was completely abject. Only when I talked about my mother did he show a spark of life. He began to weep about how he longed to be with her. Then he gave me his last cherished possession, a ring that had belonged to her. I wrapped it carefully in a handkerchief and put it in my shirt.

I visited my sister Hindah in her village, but Shivah and my three brothers met me in Shumsk and we set out together to visit my mother's grave. It pained me to see their condition. They were all pitifully thin and pale. Shivah did not hold her head up, because she was ashamed she was unmarried. What chance was there that my father would raise a dowry for her? Beryl was grown now but had no profession. Heschel had a sorrowful look to him, but the youngest, Yossel, appeared to be more rebellious. I knew he was going to ask me something, but I avoided his eyes.

At the cemetery gate, suddenly Shivah ran ahead to my mother's grave, threw herself on it, and began to weep and thrash about. I rushed to pick her up and tried to comfort her. Yossel said, "Will you send for us when you are in America?" I stood there beside that holy place and I felt calm, not dreading this request as I had before. I made a vow to them: "I promise to send for you." I did not feel weighed down, but light because I was going to do what was right. My first years in America would not be easy. I would have to work to save the fare for eight people. But why should I be afraid of hard work?

The day came when I was to leave, and Eizy drove me to the depot where other travelers had gathered. I kissed my son several times. Aaron smiled at me, unaware how long we would be separated and what it meant. Then Eizy lifted him in his arms and took him out to the wagon. Chaya and I had a few last moments. I wanted to give her something, so I gave her my mother's ring, to return to me when she saw me next. For a moment the cloud which always covered her features lifted. She embraced me and squeezed my hand hard. Then she turned to go.

The driver came in and said, "All aboard." We passengers climbed up and soon we were on the way, the horses running quickly and carrying us away from Russia and all its harshness. To what I was going, I could not know. I could only hope.

~10

I *weather some storms and do not drown*

ANTWERP, 1898

MY THOUGHTS WERE more crooked than the road. You fight for years for something, and then when you get it, you start to worry if it is the right thing. As I was traveling away, all at once I was lonely and filled with hesitations. With each verst, the decision became more wrong because it was that much more effort and expense to turn back. Although, of course, if someone ordered me to return, I would have fought against it with all my strength. What pangs it caused me to think of my wife and child and how it might be years before I saw them again. Then it occurred to me, the sooner I got to America, the harder I worked, the quicker the time would pass—so once again all my thoughts were on America, with longing.

It was an uncomfortable journey across Europe. At every border I and the other passengers had to be disinfected with kerosene. In five days I never got a chance to lie down to sleep. My bones ached. I was alway hungry, damp, or cold and usually all three together. A woman in a feathered hat scolded her husband the entire trip, reminding me of my own domestic troubles. When finally we came to Antwerp, I was so tired I was in a daze. But at least I could smell the ocean. Seagulls circled overhead and America felt close.

My hotel was not exactly luxurious, but what did I care? The landlord had a long gray beard and pouches under his eyes. We had to come to terms. He wanted me to pay two francs a week in advance. I thought it was better to pay by the night instead of the week, because I hoped my boat would leave shortly. So my rate was a little higher. I shared a room with four others, and I feasted on sleep the way a starving man at a wedding banquet stuffs himself with food. A whole night and morning went by that I slept after my arrival, and no one could get me up. In the afternoon I awoke and saw I was alone. The window was open and a breeze blew in the sooty curtains. Pushed against the walls were beds with no linens, just thin blankets. It was lonely to be in a strange city and a strange room. After I washed and got dressed, I found some writing materials and wrote to Chaya, promising her that soon she would come to a better life. I wished I could send her money for Aaron so that he would have no wants.

It was impossible to know the exact date of departure. The boats had to be packed to capacity to make the most profit, so the ship owners waited until the passenger lists were completely full. Sometimes a poor man arrived and had to wait several weeks. In that time the money he had saved to help him get started in America was used up. But it was not just the money. I was burning to get to America to prove to Chaya that I could be a success there. After wasting years, I hated wasting even a second. I loved my wife, but I had doubts that she loved me. Maybe in America . . . The sooner I began working, the better, because how else could I dispel my anxieties? But it turns out my boat was not leaving for a while, so I spent the time wandering about Antwerp.

It was an old city with many ancient buildings and a beautiful three-spired cathedral at its center. But not everything was so dignified about Antwerp. It was also a bustling port. There were sections of the city that were rough, filled with bars and brothels, where sailors loitered looking for amusements. All kinds of people arrived here and made it their home. To me it was a new experience to see yellow-skinned Chinese and dark Indians. I went about in amazement, looking in the shop windows and seeing goods that came from distant lands.

The streets were crowded with people like myself who were waiting for their boats to leave to America. There were Italians, Czechs, Turks, Poles, Lithuanians, Russians, and many others. There were the rich—women in wide satin skirts and men with ebony canes and gold watchchains across their big bellies. But the poor predominated, and the poor, it seemed to me, were mostly Jews. Everywhere were weary-looking parents with ragged children trailing after them. Every language was spoken, including the native Flemish and French, of which I could not understand a word.

I went down to the harbor to see some of the ships destined for America. I looked here and there and saw some big hulks of junk that were creaking and cracking. When I asked around, I was told these were the boats. To me it seemed impossible that such vessels could make voyages across the ocean. Yet each day they departed carrying hundreds. Hundreds more soon arrived in Antwerp. It was a never-ending flow, in and out, and of which I was a part.

On a Thursday, after five days, I left the hotel with my suitcase and packages and soon I was crowding up a gangplank with many others and onto a deck with blistering paint and rusty railings. From the deck, the crowd shoved down two flights of metal steps. Everyone was struggling to arrive first in case some advantage could be gained. But all this rushing was in vain. The lowest deck was dark. The air was stifling. Hard plank bunks hung in close rows from the walls. There were so many people pushed together that there was no room to walk about or stretch, and I saw that the ship owners were going to make a good profit on this voyage with so much "cargo," so tightly packed. At such close quarters people bickered constantly. The only peaceful ones were those who were seasick and too weak from retching, and I was one of them.

The fourth day at sea there was a violent storm. The crew and passengers from every class rushed up onto the top deck. The sky had turned black and was full of wild winds that rocked the ship. My head was turning round and round from dizziness. Green waves rose up and gushed over the sides, and meanwhile a freezing

David Toback, his wife, Chaya, and their four daughters (New York City, 1910). The author's mother is on the far right.

rain soaked everyone. People were terrified and screamed. They rushed about but were thrown down on their knees because the boat was heaving so much. The sailors lowered the lifeboats and distributed life preservers. When I saw that, the last bit of hope I had vanished. It seemed just like in Noah's time: No one could escape destruction. I said my prayers and felt a terrible sadness for myself, for all I had left undone, for the tragedy of the others who were with me, particularly the children. There was nothing to do but wait patiently. Our fate rested with the Creator. The storm continued for another two hours, then slowly the weather became calmer. The blackness gradually faded from the sky. On the horizon the sun shone weakly. The next day it was as if nothing had ever happened—just as in life, a calamity occurs, and then all trace of it is gone. Life continues.

I left the ship in New York harbor at the detention center, Castle Garden, a round red brick building which had once been a fort. I telegraphed to my uncle Heschel who lived in Manhattan. Since I had little money and no job yet, he had to come and guarantee my support before they would let me into the country. Meanwhile, as I waited for him to come, I was not idle. I waited in one line, then another, in order to be prodded and poked by doctors and interrogated by officials. Each one scribbled something on my papers.

I was escorted to a private office where a man in a crisp tan uniform looked me over. In a little while the door opened and Uncle Heschel entered. I recognized him, but with a shock. I had expected the same robust, erect person with a bristling red beard that I remembered. But now his beard was sprinkled with gray. His face was furrowed and his back bent. We tried to greet each other, but the official barked something out in English and started to interrogate my uncle. He answered quietly, then became excited and shouted. I felt alarmed. If only I understood what was being said. A policeman was summoned. He took me by the arm and began to pull me away. Heschel screamed to me in Yiddish, "Next time you come, be sure to go through Philadelphia."

I could hardly believe what I heard. Was it possible they were sending me back? I was taken down a corridor and into another room where an Italian sat with a bewildered, frightened expression. Both of us started talking at once without being understood. The guard, a big, red-faced fellow, let us know he wanted us to be quiet and not bother him. I managed, but it was difficult to sit still. Finally they brought in an interpreter and I was given an explanation.

I had unfortunately told the officials I had a wife and a child and one on the way; then my uncle came and let them know he was a poor man with a wife and six children, with another one on the way also. So the authorities reasoned, how could he guarantee me when he barely supported his own family? America did not accept beggars.

The Italian and I were taken back to the boat, and we two were the only passengers when it set sail for Europe the next day. Thank God there was no storm this time, and my sea sickness was even milder, as if I were getting accustomed to travel across the ocean. But the improvement in my accommodations did not cheer me. I would rather have been struggling with the crowd than with my unhappy thoughts. All I could think was what was I going to do now? The Italian sat opposite me with big, sad eyes and I pitied him because I knew exactly what he was suffering. Probably Chaya would say that the storm and my being sent back were signs from God that warned me not to go to America. Chaya had even dreamed about the storm. Maybe they were signs I should heed. As I swayed from one side to another with the rocking of the boat, I took one position then another. At night, neither I nor the Italian slept. We were too restless. So he played me music on a mouth organ, and I sang him prayer melodies, and even some of the shepherds' songs I had learned in Bessarabia.

Antwerp had drawn me back to itself like a magnet. I did not know the city well, and yet it seemed all too familiar as I stepped onto the dock. I settled in my old hotel where the cockroaches gave me a welcoming reception. The landlord felt sorry for me and treated me to gruel and cabbage soup. It was with the strength drawn from this nourishment that I spent an afternoon engaged in the difficult task of writing a second letter to Chaya. I had come to a decision about what to do. My intention was to fol-

low my uncle's advice and go in through Philadelphia, but this
time I would say I was unmarried. First I needed more money.
The door to America was locked, but as they say, "Gold opens all
doors."

My wife's only asset was her stingy, well-to-do brother. Could
she extract a second fare from Yisroel? Would she even try? I saw
in my mind's eye her pale face. She had fine eyebrows and a long
nose with a few freckles. For years I had stared at that face, but it
was impossible to guess her feelings. It was difficult to know exactly how she would receive the news that I had been turned back.
I struggled for hours to find the right words to move her heart and
also to think of arguments she might use to persuade Yisroel.
Never did I do work that was so exhausting. At the end sweat was
streaming down my brow. I sealed the envelope with the feeling I
was sealing my fate forever, and I said a prayer because I knew it
was only God who could help.

Later in the day I went to the *shul* where I had attended services before. People crowded around me to hear my story, and
many shook their heads and sighed. It was only because of the
members of this congregation that I was able to survive. Those
who had returned like myself always aroused pity. I found when I
came to services that a franc would be slipped into my pocket
without my even knowing. If I needed a meal, someone always invited me.

I made several friends. One man, a pious, good person, a shoemaker named Reuben Picard, I liked to visit because one of his
sons resembled Aaron. The boy was not shy with me and I could
take him up on my lap and play with him. After, I went away
more lighthearted. These were poor men like myself, but there
were a few wealthy ones in the congregation and they invited me
too. Wherever I went, the parting words of my host, whether rich
or poor, were "If you need anything, Harav David, please come to
me."

Weeks went by as I waited for Chaya's reply. I had to invent
occupations for myself. The last time I had been here, I had felt
drawn to the activity of the markets, warehouses, and stores. To
watch such things had seemed appropriate for a man with high

ambitions. Now the work of others depressed me because it reminded me of my own uselessness. I preferred to walk along the river and watch the old men fish. Or I went to a certain square where a nun would appear regularly with a big canvas bag of bread crumbs. She walked up and down and threw the crumbs out from side to side the way the peasants in my native village planted seed. The gulls shrieked in the air and they swooped down for their feast. There was also a park with gardens and fountains where I liked to sit on a bench. I had many companions there, strangers in Antwerp too with nothing to do.

One morning I went to *Ezra,* the Jewish organization which helped those who were sent back. I thought maybe I could persuade them to give me money for a new ticket, but they were only willing to help me go back to Russia. What if the authorities in Philadelphia turned me away as well? They did not want to take a chance. I banged the door furiously behind me and pushed through the crowd of new supplicants. "May you find better *ezra*° here than I did," I muttered.

I went to the park. It was the middle of July already, and the weather had become hot and humid. This added to my listlessness. Over and over I considered my predicament, but could find no way out. It was unlikely Chaya would send me money, but I could not bring myself to return. A Flemish gardener wheeled a barrow nearby and started digging in a bed of flowers. I watched him for a while. A bird sang exultantly overhead, as if there was cause for jubilation. This was painful to me and I was near tears. So you see how dejected I was? I could not forget all the indignities I had suffered in Russia, and it was terrible to think of going back. I was suffering in advance the tragedies I could expect from the future. I closed my eyes to shut out the world and my troubles.

A cool shadow fell over me. A feminine voice said in Yiddish, with a Hungarian lilt, "Hello, did you have a good sleep?" The woman was wearing a loose purple and white striped dress and twirling a parasol. Her skin was a golden color and her eyes jet-black. "Is there room for me on your bench? I was out walking and

° Help.

got tired. My name is Gittel . . . and what is yours?" She smiled at me, her teeth white and strong, except for one or two gold ones. When she sat beside me her perfume rose to my nostrils, a sweet scent, like that of the roses around us.

"What are you doing in Antwerp? Don't consider me forward. We're all strangers in this city. Which boat do you leave on?"

"I already left and came back."

She pursed her lips in sympathy. "So what are you going to do now? Do you have a wife? Children? Relatives in America?" Like a fisherman she drew the story out of me, and it relieved me to tell someone my troubles. I even began to joke, "I didn't realize it was a round-trip ticket."

"A bargain."

In the distance carriages rolled across a stone path, and ladies and gentlemen strolled. We talked a long time. She smiled a lot. I forgot to avert my eyes, and could not help noticing her dimpled cheeks, her high bosom, and her round, plump figure. I was not even aware of time going by, and she began to seem like an old friend.

"Let's get some refreshment," she suggested.

"But . . ."

"Oh, don't worry, it's my treat."

She held up a little sequined black bag which winked at me in the sunshine. Why not go with her, since I had nothing else to do? We strolled along and I felt embarrassed that I was dressed in a shabby suit. When she slipped her arm in mine, I felt embarrassed too, but I thought maybe the customs were different in Hungary. Who knows? Anyway, I was too lonely to repulse a friend.

We left the park and went down a narrow, winding street to a small hotel owned by a Jewish couple. The landlady sat in a cushioned chair in the doorway, stroking a white cat. Later she put out a saucer of milk for the cat. The landlord, a bald man with a round face, brought us some cold drinks. He sat down with us and greeted Gittel as if he had known her a long time.

"Who is this?" he asked, nodding at me.

Gittel gave me a kick under the table and I understood from this signal that I was not supposed to contradict her.

"This is my cousin."

"I see—two cousins. What a fine-looking couple. Why aren't you married?"

"My cousin lost his wife six months ago. He's ultra-orthodox, so he has to wait until the mourning period is over."

"So in a few months there will be a wedding."

"Why not?"

As soon as he had left, she whispered to me, "Don't be angry. I'll explain everything and you'll see why we have to tell people that tale."

I was upset and thinking of Chaya. It was a sin to lie, but more so to tell people my wife was dead. I could envision her reproaches—"Here, you've found a new way to hurt me."

But my companion smiled as if she had some great secret, and it made me curious. "Listen to my story and you will see it was ordained that you and I should meet." She took a tiny sip of her drink, her pink tongue darting out like the cat's. Then she suggested we move to a table in the furthest corner, so we would not be disturbed or overheard. After we had resettled ourselves, in a low voice she related the following to me.

"If you were from my area you would have heard of my father, Itzi Gershon. He has a large store and people in the whole district come to buy there. So successful he is that he has amassed thousands. And imagine, I am his only child.

"He was crazy for me. Anything I wanted he would get me. If I wanted a blue ribbon, or some sweets, or even gold earrings, all I had to do was whisper it in his ear. Then in a few weeks he would call me over and ask me to look in his jacket pocket. Whatever I wanted was there. Sometimes I had already forgotten I had asked him, because it was only a whim.

"Well, imagine when it came time for me to marry. An enormous dowry was offered, and my father was determined that I have a groom who was renowned for his learning. He did not select the groom just by himself; he called in his three brothers, and they all went around from city to city to each of the yeshivas, and asked them to bring forth their best scholars. Finally they came upon one who was considered a jewel beyond all others. The contract was signed right away, a plate broken, and only afterward did I have a chance to glance at my future husband. A shrimp with pimples on his face, cross-eyed, and stoop-shouldered. What can I say about him? I had been brought up with beautiful things around me, and everything about him repulsed me. After I took one look, I ran from the room crying, and believe me, I never stopped crying, even the day of the wedding, when they led me out and forced me to stand under the *huppa* with him. And luckily for me he was a weakling, so I could push him out of the bed. 'Let's not go on with this farce. I despise you,' I told him. He didn't say anything, but he left me alone—you understand we weren't living like man and wife.

" 'I have some money of my own, and I'll give you all of it if you'll divorce me,' I pleaded. Then I had to wait for his answer because he wanted to consider it. In a few days I heard, 'I love you, and I believe that gradually I'll be able to win you over.' The result was that I hated him more than ever. I did everything I could to spite him, so he would want to separate.

"Instead of giving me a divorce, he decided to revenge himself on me. One day he disappeared. The way he punished me was by leaving me an *agunah.* Since then, three years have passed in which I have lived without hope. I could never marry again, nor did I have a husband. Like a living grave. I never went out of the house because I didn't want people to have the satisfaction of seeing me shamed.

"Then one day I received a letter from a friend who had immigrated to America and lived in Boston. She told me she had seen my husband. The moment I read those words, I decided I'd go to America and search for him so he would divorce me. I was afraid my parents would object, so without telling anyone I gathered all the money in the house and several valuable jewels I could sell, and I too disappeared. My father is so rich that he could spare the money—and one day I would pay him back.

"The only problem was that when I came to Antwerp the ship officials refused to sell me a ticket because I was a single woman.

Now fortunately today I met you, and I believe you can help me."

"How can I be of assistance when I have already told you I have a wife and a son?"

"I don't mean, God forbid, that I'll take you away from your family. I only want to arrange a way that we can both get to America. This is my plan. We'll leave here and go to England. There we'll register as man and wife and take a boat to Boston. I'll stay in Boston and you'll travel to your uncle in New York. I want you to know that we'll travel first class, and I will pay all of your expenses."

When I hesitated, she flared up. Her face became flushed, her bosom moved up and down with anger. It made me breathless just to watch her.

"Well, I certainly don't require you in particular. I'm sure I can find someone else," she said in a sharp voice and got up to leave.

I tried to make amends. "Calm yourself; I'm not saying no. I just want a little time to think about it."

She would not hear of this. I had to decide immediately. Since I did not want this opportunity to escape me, I agreed. The wrinkles smoothed out of her face and she smiled. "Very good." Now we both got up, and the owner called after us as we went out the door, "Please invite me to the wedding."

We walked around a while longer, and when we parted I had a scrap of paper with her hotel address and an appointment for the next day. I felt troubled about this new plan until I got back to my hotel and saw that there was still no letter from Chaya. I was furious with her. The important thing was to get to America, and I decided I would put my wife and child out of my mind until I got there. Then there would be time to worry about them. Meanwhile I was really fortunate that some luck had fallen my way.

The next day I set out about noon. As I approached the area where Gittel lived, the streets became broader and the buildings better kept. I came to a corner house with turrets and a steep roof, a long, narrow building which was typical of the city. The landlady let me into a vestibule. She was a shriveled old woman with a puckered mouth and thinning gray hair which she wore tied back and tucked under a black scarf. She went to inform Gittel I had arrived. Soon Gittel came down, dressed in a light blue dress in the same flowing style as the one she had worn the day before. As she came toward me with her gliding walk, it seemed as if she were floating. "Has my cousin introduced himself?" The old woman rubbed her hands together and kept nodding and smiling as Gittel repeated the same story she had made up the day before. I could see every word was believed. Gittel announced she was taking me upstairs to her room to give me something to eat. Since we were relatives and betrothed, no objection was made.

We climbed a steep flight of steps and came to a room with narrow, high windows with flowered drapes, a bed, a table, and chairs. There was a clean smell as if the floors in the hall and the room had recently been waxed. Gittel spread a cloth on the table and put out two plates. Then she went down to the landlady's kitchen where she had some food cooking on the stove. Later, a little breathless, her face all flushed, she came carrying a tray. when she took the lid off a pot, smoke poured into the room, along with the delicious fragrance of a Hungarian-style meal of veal paprika with noodles. I savored each bite, but I noticed that she ate daintily and hardly had more than a few mouthfuls, and even these she did not seem to relish.

"How much do you pay for these quarters?" I asked.

"Ten francs," was her answer and it seemed like a fortune to me.

"When do you think we will be leaving?"

"I have been thinking about it. Before we can travel together, you will have to have a new suit. No one will believe we are husband and wife if I am well dressed and you are not. Don't worry, I will pay for everything, and as soon as the suit is ready we will travel to England and there I'll buy first-class tickets."

I blurted out, "How is it you picked me?"

"I saw you were different than the rest of the riffraff. After I talked to you a little while, I realized I did not have to look further."

This answer satisfied me, and I too did not "look further."

Before we went out, she lay down on the bed for a while to rest.

I wondered if I was getting involved with a sick woman. Why should she be so tired? Her appetite was poor, and even in the short time I had known her, I noticed she was moody, like an invalid. Or perhaps I was mistaken and the explanation was that because she came from a rich home, she was not accustomed to exerting herself with cooking. I made these reflections as I looked out the window. This hotel was near the diamond district, and I saw a few messengers going by carrying the black sacks they'd take back and forth between the diamond-cutting workshops and which were full of gems.

"Come, let's go." Gittel was on her feet and putting on her hat, a straw one with a green band and cherries on it. Soon we were hurrying through the streets to the tailor's shop, a small place made cramped by the bolts of material that were piled high, up to the ceiling. The tailor began measuring me, while Gittel examined the cloth and at the same time haggled over the price. By the time she had selected something, the tailor had finished measuring, and the only thing that was not decided was when the suit would be ready. First he said three weeks, then two, but Gittel begged, and at last he said he would "*try* for one"—but earlier than that was impossible. So when we left the tailor's shop we knew we had a week to pass in Antwerp.

She was lonely, and so was I, so we spent most of our time together and discussed our futures in America. We sat in her room talking, played cards, or went for walks. Once she even hired a carriage and we went out to the countryside with a hamper of food. The landscape was flat and green. It stretched to the sea and there was an occasional windmill or thatched cottage. Not a cloud was in the sky. I wore a new shirt and cap she had bought me, and it was a pleasant day. The only difficulty was that Gittel tired easily, and we had to go back after a few hours.

A number of people in Antwerp were acquainted with me by this time, and it was difficult to go through the streets without someone recognizing me. Gittel was afraid I was going to endanger her chance of getting to America by blurting out our secret. She wanted me to take all my meals with her, so I would not go to people's houses. At the *shul* I informed everyone that I had received some money. From now on I would not be coming to anyone for meals because I did not have to take charity any longer. Anyway, they should say good-bye to me, because I was leaving Antwerp any day now. A few of my friends wanted to question me further, but I did not linger after the services.

Even though I took my meals with her, I had to reassure Gittel constantly that I had revealed nothing. She said I had an open nature and someone could see by the expression on my face that I was lying. This anxiety never left her, only grew, particularly when the tailor was late with the suit and it turned out we would have to wait at least an extra week after all. This news so upset Gittel that she started to cry as we left the tailor's shop. "It's only one week," I said to comfort her, and she calmed down a little. She kept a lace handkerchief in her bodice and she took it out and dried her eyes. We walked along. Overhead large clouds formed, and I hoped it would rain to relieve the heat. Our clothes were sticking to us and we could barely move.

My friend Reuben, the shoemaker from the *shul*, came walking toward us from the opposite direction. He recognized me and came over. When he saw I was with a woman he cried out, "Ah, instead of a letter, your wife came herself."

"No, this isn't my wife," was all I could manage, but Gittel came to my rescue.

"I'm his cousin."

She seemed a shade paler and her eyes were flashing.

"Now all of a sudden you have a cousin?"

"We have to go," Gittel said.

"But why are you running off, David? When are you coming to visit again? My son Shmuel misses you. He asks me and my wife where you are and we don't know."

Before I could answer, Gittel pulled me around the corner. My last sight of Reuben was his look of astonishment.

"I didn't like that man."

"Why? He's a kind person."

"He looks like he's too curious about other people's business."

"He's just worried about me. Why should I lie to someone who has been so good to me? If I told him the truth, he could keep it quiet."

"When three know, there's no secret!"

"And anyway, why did you pull me away like that? That would really make him curious."

I could see she was alarmed. Finally she said, "I'm going to have to watch over you constantly. In fact, there's a room free on another floor of my hotel and you will move in there. We will spend all our time indoors."

"I have to go to services at the *shul.*"

"You can pray in your room for these few days."

"Is that right? I should pray with a *minyan.*"

She began to cry that because of me she would lose her chance to get a divorce from her husband. We argued a bit, but in the end I went to my hotel and got my belongings.

At dinner I was merry. Gittel filled my glass to the brim with wine several times. I laughed a lot. I drank so much that I dozed off in my seat. When I woke, I saw she had cleared the dishes away and was sitting by the window looking out. Finally it had begun to rain. Lightning streaked the sky. A few moments later the roll of thunder was heard. There was a distorted expression on Gittel's face, but even more than that my attention was caught by her hands. One was resting just below her breasts and the other a little lower. The fingers were spread out and pressing hard against her body as if she was trying to squeeze a ball beneath the skin. I said to myself that she was not well enough to travel across the ocean. Probably she and I would not go to America. Something else I was trying to figure out too. I was squeezing my brain hard, just the way she was pressing her belly—but what it was I had to know I could not grasp.

The thunder started again. Gittel turned slowly toward me. I saw she was surprised I was awake. She stared at me as if she was trying to look into my thoughts. She seemed different to me, although I did not know in what way. A smile came to her lips and she rose and came slowly toward me. I was surprised when she brought her hand to my face and stroked my cheek.

"I'm glad you came to stay here. Now we can be together," she said huskily.

I started to tremble.

"I've been waiting for you to make the first move. Why don't you act like a man?" Before I could answer, her lips brushed mine. All Torah was erased from my mind. No man can fight his body; no man can destroy the animal that is in him. I was burning with a fire that had to be quenched. We went to the bed, and we lay with each other. Gittel and Chaya became mixed up, became one person. It was Chaya's hands, her large, bony hands that caressed me; it was Gittel's mouth that moaned. It was Chaya's eyelids that fluttered. It was Gittel's shoulder I bit. We fell apart exhausted, our bodies throbbing, my mind blank, like an animal's. Then slowly the pain and sadness in me began to build. I had lusted after my wife too without there being love between us. It had been the same now as then—and maybe the one made the other happen.

I turned and gazed at Gittel, who lay beside me naked. She became aware of my eyes on her and hastily covered herself with the sheet, but not before I saw her secret. Her clothes had been able to conceal the swelling, which was not too great yet. She was about six months pregnant. The story she had told me about herself was completely false, or at least she had left out a lot. She murmured, "Go to sleep." I pretended to sleep. When she had rolled on her side and was breathing deeply, I got up quietly, dressed, and went outside.

I began to walk around without knowing where I was going. For hours I walked. Up ahead I saw some lighted windows and moved toward them like a moth to a candle. I had gooseflesh when I saw what was in these windows. In the first sat a redheaded woman with green eyes and milk-white skin; she was naked to the waist. In the next was a fat woman whose nakedness was covered only by a light shawl. She had long, hanging breasts and she held them out, beckoning with her hand and spreading her huge thighs. She started to laugh, and her mouth opened to expose rotting teeth.

I ran away. I did not know where to go, so I went back to my old hotel. Maybe I could get my old room back. I could not return to the place where I had defiled myself, not even to get my luggage. When I came in, no one was around but an old man with a thin gray beard, little eyes, and a rumpled black yarmulke. He was bent over a big Talmud and reading. I saw it was *Nashim*, the order on women in the Mishnah. I wanted to fall to the floor with shame. Finally I asked the old man where the landlord was. He cocked his hand to his ear. The more I shouted, the more deaf he was. It was as if whatever came from my mouth was impure and such a holy man would not hear my words. I gave up and sat down and waited for the landlord to show up. Once again I thought maybe I should never have left Russia. Chaya had warned me. Even before I got to America I was corrupted—and what would happen when I was there? I should go back to *Ezra* and get the fare. This idea, though, made me sick to my stomach. But where should I go? At last the landlord came and greeted me: "I've been looking for you all day. You got a letter."

I took it from him and went to the lamp to read. It was in my wife's handwriting. It seemed to me that she was hidden in the shadows of the room. I felt her presence. She had black eyes like Gittel's, but they seemed duller because they were half-lidded and looking inward. Tears came to my eyes when I saw that inside the envelope was a money order for the ticket to Philadelphia. The reason there was so much delay was because she had traveled around and collected from a number of people. She wrote, "Go to America if it is the only way your soul can find peace. But please send for me as soon as you can. I cannot live without you." She had never spoken to me with such passion as in her last words. I felt as if I did not know her at all, but now I was certain of her love.

Why had I not put my faith in her and waited? There was a blot on my life that I would never erase. Still, as I read her letter, I felt as if I was healed from a sickness that had been sapping me for years. I was renewed. I had strength now to walk a straight path, and to survive all the hardships ahead.

Not wanting to meet Gittel again, I went as soon as possible to Southampton in England. There I got a ship to Philadelphia. When I got to America they let me in with no difficulty. The old world had finally let me go.

For whom have I written all this?

IT IS HARD for me to believe that all these places I remember are now no more. My father-in-law had prophesied that everything would be destroyed, and he was right.

In 1903, with the blessings of Nicholas II, there was a terrible pogrom in Kishinev. When I wrote to Neci and Yankel, I got no answer; so I mourned them as I would a mother and father.

One night I had an unusual dream about my Aunt Bobbah, that she was stretched out on a table dressed in a green velvet gown with sable trim, and she was smiling peacefully. Only a few months after this I heard how Semosenko led his cossacks into Proskurov to slaughter the Jews. His excuse was that he believed they were all Bolsheviks. In pogroms before this, the Jews had been looted and murdered, but not deliberately tortured. The Proskurov pogrom set a new example. Parents were forced to watch their children torn apart bit by bit; cats were sewn into the stomachs of old women. Every abomination was committed.

The thought of a saintly old man like Israel the healer being tormented is horrifying, yet I imagine he had more fortitude than my Aunt Bobbah. It is worse to think what she suffered, poor woman. Just the scowling expression that was natural to her face must have aroused a group of cossacks to a frenzy. Surely all her sins were atoned through her agonies. Uncle Nuchem and she both perished.

My father is dead, but there are others in Shumsk for whom I care. My sister Hindah and her family moved there. The town is occupied by the Nazis and no word comes. Will the killers permit a single Jewish soul to escape?

I left behind Death. All my misfortunes in Russia were blessings because they gave me the strength to leave. By emigrating I am sure I saved my life.

I arrived here in 1898 when I was twenty-three years old. I lived with my uncle and worked at his shop. I joined a *shul* at 32 Orchard Street, but was dissatisfied. The rich members sat up high on a couch where the *hazzan* sang. Better to leave such customs behind with the czar. They didn't belong in a democracy. Those who attempted to object were not permitted to have a say.

Six of us got together and decided we did not need the "holy vessels" on the couch. We were able to gather forty members, and we said good-bye to 32 Orchard and moved to 20 Orchard Street where there was all the difference in the world. We did not know about special privileges. Everyone was called up to read Torah.

We had a *Hevra Kaddisha*, but unlike the other *shuln*,* our emphasis was on the living. A charitable society was begun which we wanted to be a model for our countrymen, to teach them what an organization demands from its members. Health benefits were paid, and we provided nursing care for each other.

When I myself became ill, two men in the congregation came to care for me. I was happy. I said, "Now I observe the fruits of my labor."

I was working long hours pressing boys' pants and carrying heavy loads up and down stairs, and I saved every penny to bring over my wife and children. But what happened was that my brothers wrote me they were going to get drafted, and it was possible the military would keep them for as long as thirty years. I felt I had no choice, that I had to send them all the money I had and

* Plural of *shul.*

*David at 67 and Chaya on vacation in Mountaindale, New York (1942),
the year his granddaughter, Carole Malkin, was born.*

bring them over here first. I sent for Beryl and then Heschel, and those two brought over Yossel and Shivah.

I started saving again. Two years went by, and it would take another two. In Russia I had a daughter Tzerl, whom I had never seen, and I longed for her. She was born a half year after my departure. Time passed and the money started to accumulate. My brothers came to me with a proposition—they wanted to start their own clothing factory and they needed my savings to buy sewing machines.

Heschel said, "Why should we let our uncle go around all puffed up that he does us a favor?"

My answer was, "I can't delay sending for my wife a second time."

"But it will be better for her—you'll be a businessman. She'll thank you that you got settled well and didn't bring her over to poverty."

"I'm lonely without my wife and children."

"Don't be selfish. A woman doesn't want to come to such a poor situation. You're passing up a good investment. Besides, you are the oldest brother and are supposed to help us."

They never left me alone. Every moment was filled with their pleading. I decided to put an end to it by wiring all the money to Chaya. When my brothers heard, they wouldn't talk to me for a long time. They quit my uncle's and went to work in a union shop that had shorter hours and higher pay. After a while they did go into their own business. They were good workers but didn't have ability as managers, and soon they lost everything—so that's what would have become of my "good investment."

My wife telegraphed me she was coming. I went to Castle Garden and when I searched for her in the crowd, I looked right past her. I was trying to find a young woman, but the one who rushed forward had lost her youth. How Chaya clung to me and cried. Her first words were, "My husband, do you still speak Yiddish?" I took her and the children to the room I had just rented. Aaron, eight years old already, was brave and ran out to explore everything. Chaya sat on the edge of the bed as if it were contaminated. I wanted to get to know three-year-old Tzerl, but she held on to her mother and started to shriek. The neighbor came in and tried to be friendly, but my wife was shy. Her face was downcast, never cheerful. She got the reputation for being proud.

Chaya said she couldn't cook because nothing here was kosher, and to a great extent she was right. In Europe the Jews fooled goyim by pouring water into brandy and giving short weight, but here Jews fooled other Jews and passed off *treyf* as kosher. Suddenly rabbis had to have licenses and there had to be inspectors, and even then who knew what was pure?

A piece of meat never passed my wife's lips, and she ate little of anything else. She started getting all kinds of illness. Her lips cracked. She was dizzy. One time she fainted at the grocery. I saw she was thinner and thinner, and so was my daughter, as if Tzerl had to suffer everything with her mother.

Each morning I went to work at the shop with a heavy heart, afraid to return to find an ambulance at my house. I would come in and the lights would be off, and my wife and Tzerl just sat there in darkness. Aaron came in and talked to his mother in a surly way. I think he wanted to see some life in her. Better she should be angry than acting like a dead person. I scolded him, but not much. Often, I myself had to prepare the evening meal.

One night I met Napthali, one of those who had helped found the *shul* at 20 Orchard Street.

"David," he said, "I beg you to help me. My relatives just came off the boat and have nowhere to stay. My wife has a contagious disease and no one is permitted in the house."

"My wife can't have guests either."

"Please, just for one night. Can I put my cousins out on the street?"

I felt we in the congregation should never refuse one another a favor. This was a principle with me, and so finally I agreed and "for just one night" I brought home a young couple with a small baby. The wife was no more than sixteen. Chaya was furious, but when she saw this girl sitting in the corner and crying, she took pity. She went and held her in her arms. Who could understand better what she was suffering?

As a result of that evening our life together changed. Chaya had found her task in life. She took on as her special job welcoming the women who had just arrived from Europe. There was hardly a time when we were not sharing our small quarters with another family. I never objected. I was glad because Chaya was a changed woman, active, bustling around. And if she had a sharp tongue, what did I care? At least she wasn't depressed.

Tzerl was still a melancholy child, as if she had suckled all Chaya's worries with her mother's milk. My wife never had to reprimand her that she was noisy or that she soiled her clothes. We had three more children—all daughters—and Tzerl sat to one side and watched as they played. She was always so timid that she couldn't help my wife take care of them. If Tzerl would have given an order, they would have laughed or pulled her hair—but Tzerl never gave an order, only watched with her large gray eyes.

The other children were more lively, but she was the beautiful one. When she was only fifteen years old, she would walk down the street and people held their breath and forgot where they were. I worried, what would become of such a child? But like the others, she went to high school, and she got married and had children.

Tzerl, did you think you were an angel? One day you had to climb up to the edge of the roof and fly away.

I have to wipe the tears from my eyes so they don't stain the page.

My wife is sitting across from me shelling peas for our dinner. Does she notice I am crying? She clears her throat and moves around in her chair and seems to be struggling for something to say.

Then she addresses me in a croaking voice. "Be careful what you write, my husband. . . . Don't mention any names. You might offend someone."

"How is it possible someone will be offended? A thousand times I told you, no one will read."

"Then why are you wasting your time?" she flares up and goes into one of her long speeches that remind me of her parents. My heart softens to her, because she knows what I have been thinking about and she distracts me in the only way she knows.

But she is right. Now that I am coming to the end, I have to consider, what was the significance of filling all these notebooks?

Will anyone be interested to read? In America people don't care about an old person and his memories. I have a nephew who changed his name from Silverstein to Sterling.

If I phone, his secretary says, "Mr. Sterling is out," or "Mr. Sterling is too busy to talk."

This is because he's a manager at Smith's Department Store. I understand also he's joined a club in which Jews are not permitted as members. How does this manager manage that? It seems he doesn't want to remember who his relatives are.

So for whom have I written all this?

I'm going to put it all in the closet, and when I die it goes into the garbage. And yet if there is one thing I have learned well in my life, it is that "the wheel turns." All that is required is patience. My youngest daughter Miriam has recently given birth to a son. Perhaps my new grandson . . .

✒ AFTERWORD

"Where can great treasures be found in America?
One must search and search and then
possibly one can be found in a trashcan."

DAVID TOBACK

SEVERAL YEARS AGO my grandfather's handwritten Yiddish memoir came into my hands. Translation of the memoir was begun in 1973 by Kenneth Blady and took two and a half years to complete. The translated work proved to be a great treasure of authentic tales which I decided to retell and set into a narrative which would connect them more integrally.

The stories my grandfather wrote down were ones he probably told again and again. Like all good storytellers, he might have even acted out various parts. He had a superb ear for dialogue, and much of the dialogue I use is taken intact from the translation of the Yiddish memoir.

I saw my task as selecting, organizing, and filling in those areas that were missing and were needed to form a coherent and dramatic narrative. To achieve this I did research in books and made a visit to the Soviet Union. I also used my imagination in writing about some of David's thoughts, perceptions, and feelings.

I worked with only a portion of the original five notebooks, leaving out material which did not enhance or fit smoothly into the general narrative. For instance there were long sections which listed David's diet from day to day. It is a poignant indication of the poverty he experienced that he would remember to mention a piece of bread, an apple, or a cookie. Nonetheless, such lists make for tedious reading.

It was sometimes necessary to reset and vary events in ways that would permit clearer elucidation of David's life and character. The original memoir gave few details about people's names and appearance or the physical settings of the places David visited. In such cases I supplied them, based on my research of the period. As the narrative drew closer to the present, I wanted to protect the privacy of people who are still alive and fictionalized in a way which would achieve this. Episodes are somewhat changed and expanded for dramatic effect.

In sum, I have used a certain amount of poetic license. I wanted to bring the notebooks to life and form them into a polished whole, and while doing so I tried to be as faithful as possible to the soul that first animated them.

A page from the original memoir by David Toback.
Reprinted by permission of the Jewish National Library, Israel.

Acknowledgments

WHEN I BEGAN the task of writing a book based on the memoir, I was enrolled at San Francisco State University as a graduate student in Creative Writing. I had the opportunity to receive critical assistance on this project from Mr. William Dickey, the chairman of the department at the time. More than anyone else, he helped me to understand the various dimensions of the manuscript and spurred me to bring it to completion. I wish to thank him for being a perceptive, sensitive, and encouraging critic. I am also grateful to my friend Konstantin Berlandt, who read sections of the book with intelligence and painstaking care, and to my husband, Richard Malkin, for his suggestions and for always being a willing and helpful audience, even through many drafts of the book.

To several others I wish to express my gratitude. I took a course from Dr. Irving Halperin entitled "The American Jewish Writer" and one from Dr. Dov Noy, "The Jewish Life Cycle." Both courses deepened my understanding of my grandfather's experiences. Dr. Noy assisted me in locating certain Russian cities and towns on maps. I entrusted the original memoir to him to take to Hebrew University in Jerusalem.

The spring issue of *Davka*, 1977, contains a story I wrote from the point of view of David's father, Leibish Hershik, and which concerns the wonder-working rabbis in Russia. I am grateful for the encouragement received from the editor, Neil Reisner.

Harry Shukman and Martin Gilbert of Oxford University, England, were helpful in showing me drawings and photographs of the period in which I was interested and making research suggestions.